The Document Matters

ABC Group Documentation //
878 Mallory Drive
Marietta, GA 30062

ISBN: 978-1-64396-238-2

Printed in the USA.

COOL IT DOWN

by

Alec Cizak

"An ant cannot move a tree"
-Chinese idiom

Hi Kids!

He could never recall the exact age. Three? Four? His father, perhaps feeling guilty for having spanked him the first of countless times, brought home a Mickey Mouse record player. It looked like a plastic suitcase until opened. The famous rat had been drawn onto the underside of the cover in a sky blue and white-striped T-shirt. His gloved hand served as the arm, the needle hidden under a single, pointing finger. His father called him in to the living room, told him to have a seat on thin, unraveling carpet. Mickey Mouse's giant face grinned at them as his father unwound the power cord and plugged it in. He said, "Know what this is?" After sifting through a collection near his stereo system, his father returned with an album sheathed in a cardboard sleeve adorned with an illustration of stairs descending to a subway. Pink clouds emerged from wherever the steps led to, as though someone were smoking a very special kind of cigarette in the dark. There were words written in puffy, friendly letters. His father said, "Every song is perfect." He pulled out a black, vinyl disc several sizes larger than the turntable. His father dropped the needle on the third groove. A lively tune played on the tiny speakers mounted on the underside of the suitcase. Someone named Jenny seemed dissatisfied with her life until she heard a radio station from New York. The singer went on to suggest Jenny's life had been *saved by rock and roll.*

His father patted him on the shoulder. "Let me see how your mother's doing." He left him with the record player and the story of the disgruntled amputee insisting she could still dance. Something happened. Something he would spend his life pondering without verbalizing it, without visiting a psychologist and paying an unholy amount of money for conference with clergy of a different cloak. Because he knew, if *he* didn't understand what had happened next, no one would. Perhaps he recognized the record player as a bribe, offered by, at that point in his life, the most powerful human being in the universe, with the intention of smoothing over the previous night's violent episode:

As always, his father had come home from work tired and grumbling. Much like the girl in the song, his father never seemed happy with his life. He often complained and barked at his mother. She yelled back, equally displeased with her fate. Arguments ensued at the dinner table. Before that, however, his father would sit in a reclining comforter in the living room and watch the only television in the house. He would catch a rerun of *M.A.S.H.* and settle in for Walter Cronkite's account of the day's relevant catastrophes. Upon his mother's instructions, he would summon his father for dinner. For whatever reason, the night before his father had brought home the Mickey Mouse record player, he'd decided to play a joke on him. He told him to come to dinner before his mother had finished cooking. Learning of this deceit, his father had taken off his belt and whipped him on his backside until his legs numbed. He then told him to stand in the corner and contemplate his dishonesty.

Well, he must not have wanted a payoff. He must have wanted a straight apology. He must have known the old man had no business beating him the way he did. He smacked the record player and Mickey Mouse's arm scratched across the surface of the record. A hideous noise filled the room, like brakes on a car squealing to a halt. The needle damaged the record. It caught on a broken groove and the singer repeated, *Death of us, death of us, death of us,* over and over and over, like one of those funny birds at the zoo, birds with colorful feathers and the ability to repeat simple, mindless human chatter. His father charged into the room from the kitchen. "What the hell?" He kneeled and yanked Mickey Mouse's arm off the record. He looked at his son and said, "What the hell is wrong with you?" Unable to provide a response, unaware of why he'd done what he had done, he shrugged. His father's left hand landed backward across his face, his wedding ring slicing into his lip. He used the sleeve of his Cookie Monster sweatshirt to pat his blood.

The most powerful man in the universe stood, tears in his eyes, and said, "I do something nice for you, and this is how you repay me?"

One

There comes a point, traveling the 75 corridor in Florida, where boredom becomes unbearable, compels a driver to pull off at the next town and be done with it. Nothing but dark, army green trees on both sides. Little variation. Occasional, scattered palms. Blake Ness, fleeing New Orleans, fleeing a woman who'd promised to kill him, had hoped to spot saurian monsters lounging in the drainage ditches. It had been ten hours since he'd left Mobile, stopping only to take a leak, fill the tank on his dying Renault Escort, and grab a veggie sandwich at a gas station sub shop. He passed Tampa, figuring a larger city an easy place for the woman from New Orleans to find him. He pulled off at Bradenton, didn't see anything appealing, and crawled through the crowded streets of Sarasota until a billboard towering over Tamiami announced, *Cool it Down on Raro Key!* Next to the Tiki-styled writing, a tanned blonde in a bikini rested on the back of a grinning alligator. She sipped from a straw, her lips adorned with blinking, ruby sparkles. Beneath the woman and the reptile, plain text directed anyone interested to turn at the next stoplight.

Blake crossed a steel, meshed drawbridge to the island. A swamp bubbled to his right, oatmeal-colored bungalows lined the shores to his left. Yachts bobbed in their slips at wooden docks, their masts nodding like metronomes. He thought of Mrs. Ciao, his piano teacher from seventh grade. She let the damn tick-tock grate on whether he needed guidance or not. She'd crash the bottoms of her wrinkled, soggy fists into his fingers any time he hit foul notes. His parents, who'd forced him to study the instrument, couldn't figure out why he had no desire to practice and improve. When Mrs. Ciao informed them their son could not be trained, they thanked her. Blake's father decided a beating would compensate for the financial loss.

"Got to love the middle class." Blake spoke to the silent radio in the center of the dashboard of his worn car. He'd picked up the Renault in Kentucky. The dealer took cash, asked no dangerous questions, and sold him a registration and license plate listed under the name Blake eventually assumed. The dealer said the name belonged to a dead man whose expiration had been overlooked by county bureaucrats. "Radio work?" he asked. The dealer shrugged, his oversized sportscoat bouncing off his shoulders like useless wings. First time the calendar turned, Blake sold the car to the woman from New Orleans. Despite her side-job with a local crime family, her official record remained clean. She went to the DMV in Metairie and learned the '88 Renault qualified for a classic plate, which meant it would never have to be registered again.

He merged onto a narrow, winding road called Moonlight Pass. Cars heading in opposite directions swerved to avoid collisions. Date palms crowded thin bands of dirt pretending to be sidewalks. Their leaves sprouted like fireworks. He'd expected retirees and families to populate the island, but saw only young people, most of whom appeared destitute, dressed in baggy clothes and torn, shoddy swimsuits. Every woman, it seemed, had white-girl dreadlocks and tattoos. The men tied their hair into buns on the tops of their heads. Blake suspected their unkempt lumberjack beards convinced them the modern world had *not* drained their testosterone. The few women who noticed him made eye contact and smiled. Nice enough. He could tolerate hippies while he decided just how far south he'd go to make sure the woman from New Orleans never found him.

The road widened at the ocean. A small block of businesses occupied a three-story, red-bricked joint across from the beach—a diner called Deep Fried Heaven; Vinyl Destination, a record store; a building the size of a waiting room in a doctor's office, designated as Trascendente; and Let's Chill, a massage parlor, from the looks of the medical posters in the windows and neon *Open* sign in the door.

Blake pulled into the parking lot at the beach and searched for a spot. The air, cooling as a blood-colored sun melted into the horizon, thumped to a tribal rhythm traveling from the direction of the ocean. He found a place between two Japanese CRVs. Sliding out a shoebox filled with cash from under the passenger seat, he grabbed a few hundred bucks, stuffed the bills into his pocket, and returned the stash to its hiding place. His toes itched. He took off his shoes and socks and rolled up his slacks. He'd worn a button-down shirt, open, over a plain, white T-shirt. He removed the button-down shirt and tossed it onto the passenger seat. Once upon a time, he would never have walked in public in just a T-shirt. Once upon a time, he'd been a bloated, self-loathing working class schmuck. He'd poisoned himself with fast food and television. Liberation from that life, courtesy a heap of stolen money, allowed him time and space needed to transform, to become someone entirely new. He stopped paying for fast food and learned how to cook his own, healthy meals. Within days, he no longer felt like shit. Then he began a basic exercise routine. Every morning—stretching, squats, push-ups, sit-ups. Nothing strenuous. His odometer rolled over to forty the year before and he felt no need to tax himself. This relaxed, disciplined approach evicted blubber he'd carried like a toxic halo around his waist for twenty years. His skin tightened across lean muscle and he morphed from schlub to a man women looked at twice.

The asphalt had yet to receive word of the sun's retreat. He jumped a couple of times on his way to the sand as pebbles poked his heels. He stopped for a drink of water at a fountain near a concrete arch with restrooms and a bar. Blazing orange letters hanging over the entrance announced, Lonesome Cowboy Bill's. Game trophies decorated the walls. Multicolored Christmas lights illuminated the outer edges of the joint. The patrons looked, for the most part, middle-aged. Blake's age. Gravity had turned them into caricatures. They dressed the same, carried the same lines in their faces, like death loitered around them, occasionally slashing at them with the tip of its scythe, carving ravines into the crevices outlining their eyes, noses, and mouths. Perhaps, to some, he may have looked no different. He couldn't tell. Family, mortgages, *responsibilities*, these things didn't sit on his shoulders, swelling with time. He followed a group of young women dressed in cloth bikinis past a wall of bushes to white sand stretched across the shoreline. The women headed toward a crowd gathered around torches and a dozen drummers. The sun cast them in a candy apple glow. They danced as they walked, their hips twitching in rhythm with the drums. Light wind brushed the land and Blake Ness believed, right then, in the idea of heaven. The necessity of faith in a reward for a life well-lived, he decided, granted the ability to wake up every morning and give the Great Tragedy another chance. Yes, it made no sense, according to science, or European voodoo, as the woman from New Orleans called it, to think a total shutdown of all biological faculties led to anything but oblivion. But it didn't matter. When the Reaper came for him, Blake would be here, on the hot sand, chasing beach bunnies in bikinis, their goofy naval piercings, their tramp stamps, beckoning him, delivering an eternity of the *promise* of pleasure, a teasing of the senses surpassing, in some ways, the joy of finally catching and conquering a beautiful woman.

He arrived at the drum circle and weaved into the crowd of onlookers. The drummers had arranged themselves in a wedge with their backs toward the parking lot and a patch of swampland darkened by crooked trees resembling curled, protective fingers. Torches had been arranged in an eight-point star and topless women in cream-colored thongs drew red circles in the air with burning batons. The drumming increased, the ground rumbled. Opposite the drummers, an adult-sized sheep had been chained to a stake in the sand. It bleated and yanked its head, trying to free itself. It bent its front legs and bucked. The tether must have been anchored deep. It slammed the animal's head against the ground, calming it, for a moment. Blake took in the people around him. They reeked of marijuana, patchouli, and body odor. Women with unwashed hair whipped around musky scents like altar servants clouding a church with incense from swinging censers. He wanted to ask about the sheep. The women flailed their arms and shook. Possessed. He opted not to interrupt their union with the rhythm. While he suspected them nothing more than wealthy runaways, he appreciated their attempts to establish something, *anything* spiritual. The masses, even those attending services every Sunday, seemed to have abandoned the pursuit of understanding their place within the universe. He had once been similar, a nihilist, finding no purpose in life beyond mocking it. Nothing more than veiled masochism. Led only to misery, depression. The woman from New Orleans had steered him to a better path.

The crowd on the other side of the circle separated, created space for something emerging from the swamp. The sun sat in a single, sloppy layer on the horizon. The purple cool of night and a half moon winking at the Earth painted the creature crawling toward the circle in shadow. Soon, shimmying, orange torchlight cast a strobing reveal over an alligator as big as a station wagon marching bowlegged, like a bulldog, its tail gliding side-to-side. Not much scared Blake since his escape from his previous life, but he could not stop himself from taking a step backward, sand tickling the spaces between his toes, as the gator huffed at the crowd, as if to suggest they make room. The sheep sounded psychotic in its panicked bleating, calling out, perhaps, to its concept of a Grand Creator for mercy. The alligator's mouth closed as it turned to face the sheep. It lowered itself and approached the sheep at a cautious pace, as though it believed the weaker animal might design a method to snap its chains and flee. The drumming achieved thunderous volume. The alligator leapt the final feet between it and the sheep, its scissor-jaws crashing onto the sheep's neck and twisting and tearing as it pinned the weaker animal to the sand and ripped off its head.

The hippies snapped their fingers like beatniks in a coffee house. The alligator munched on the sheep's decapitated torso. Blood and wool danced in the air, decorating the beast's mouth like some macabre Christmas display at a shopping mall. The sheep's detached head rolled to the side of the gator. Its mouth moved, perhaps delivering its own last rites. When the alligator had turned the sheep's torso into a slop of pink gore dripping off slick, collapsed bone fragments, it tilted its jaws sideways and scooped up the sheep's head and swallowed it in one gulp. It strolled back into the darkness, its tail swerving with a decelerated, hushed rhythm the drummers mimicked. Blake put his hand over his stomach. The veggie sub he'd eaten earlier threatened to vacate. His belly turned at the thought of using the public restroom under the concrete arch. Even worse, however, would be throwing up in front of all those people. What others thought of him hadn't mattered much, even when he'd been a loser. But he didn't want to appear spineless in front of a tribe of hippies entertained by animals destroying each other.

Two

A sleek, flat-screen television had been mounted above the bar in Lonesome Cowboy Bill's. A newscaster read a headline regarding the latest roadside tragedy between a pale-faced police officer and a motorist with darker skin. Dashcam video showed a young man fleeing flashes of smoke and collapsing out of frame. The broadcast cut back to a woman behind a slick, canary desk, now identified by a title overlay as Linda Lee. Her straight, black hair had been tied into a ponytail wagging with each dramatic twitch her left nostril offered to punctuate the sordid story. She had caramel-colored skin and what old-timers called sleepy eyes, compelling Blake to fathom the possibility of bedding Ms. Linda Lee. Perched high on a wooden stand near the television, a rainbow-colored parrot situated and resituated itself. On occasion, it would repeat what Linda Lee said on the television, bowing its head and blurting out in a raspy voice, *Racist, racist, clearly racist*, like Rain Man, if Rain Man smoked a thousand cigarettes a day.

The men in the bar sported the official Florida uniform— Hawaiian shirt, cargo shorts, and sandals. The women tried harder to separate themselves, some in skirts, some in pleated pants. If they felt comfortable showing more of their legs, they did. Some had left one button too many undone on their blouses, allowing the pre-geezer crowd a charitable view of their cleavage. Blake held gaze with women confident enough to smile and mean it. The men complemented dismissive shrugs with defeatist grunts.

They must have detected, here stood a man who had not buttered and browned his lips for a weekly pittance, a man who'd wormed out of the system and, somehow, *not* wound up at the door of a convenience store, pleading for spare change. The woman from New Orleans called it spite. She'd brought it up the first time they'd gone out to eat and a decrepit white woman glared at them with ancient, tribal fury. Whom did she hate more, the black woman on Blake's arm, or Blake, the race traitor? He'd said, "How about I stick my foot up her ass and tie my shoes through her goddamn nose?" The woman from New Orleans told him to settle down.

"You're living a life she can't," she'd said. "It's not prejudice she's projecting. It's *spite*." She'd gripped his hand, brought her legs under the table up and around his hips. "Imagine being so small-minded. Why give her grief when God's already punished her?"

And, of course, she'd been correct. Most people had to play The Game. The system would fail if they didn't. They were conditioned from childhood to stand in line, to wait their turn, to do as told. Grade school teachers administered the first lessons in conformity— keep your pencil on one side of the desk, your eraser on the other. Sit straight. Don't giggle on the walk to the cafeteria. Boys compete at kickball on the playground. Girls jump rope. Get a job. Get married. Consume garbage advertised on television. Make babies. Make sure they behave the exact same way. Those who were slightly ornery, those who wandered out on a limb every now and then and talked back, punched back, they fell into the working class. They didn't want to starve, so they took rough jobs to keep the frailest roofs over their heads. Those who refused to give the system the slightest show of respect had two options:

Beg.

Steal.

The twists and turns in Blake's life had led him to the last choice. And it paid off. Not a story Hollywood would ever have the guts to tell. He'd robbed a man of obscene wealth and he'd killed a child molester known as Uncle Sewell. He'd pulled into the gravel lot outside Uncle Sewell's ranch house, loaded his belly pistol with fresh rounds, and marched up the zig-zag front walk. The single-story house had been painted bright cherry. Well-kept gardens of red and yellow roses flanked the slim stoop leading to the door. Crude paintings of Raggedy Ann and Andy pranced in a circle around the knocker, holding hands just over the weathered, brass hinge. Blake lifted the square knocker and slammed it into the sturdy, wooden door twice. Then he stepped back, his hand in his jacket, his finger curled around the trigger guard. As floorboards inside the house creaked, he regretted his decision. He'd told himself to expect such a reaction. He couldn't stop his heart from beating faster, his fingers from moistening with sweat. He imagined sliding the gun from his pocket, aiming, and his finger slipping, causing the bullet to stray. No telling if the owner of the house answered the door armed, if he might shoot first. He wanted to turn around and leave. And then the door opened. Standing in the shadows of a long, front hallway, a tall, flimsy man resembling a Nazi officer ducked his head outside. He leered at Blake the way Blake ogled women at strip clubs. The man sneered, as though he'd surmised Blake Ness's biography up to that point and found it unimpressive. What a relief that had been. Blake remembered, right then, this man had destroyed Chelsea Farmer, a young woman he'd been in love with; Yes, he'd been an idiot for chasing after her in the first place. The young woman's fickle nature scorned him, compelled him to do things to her beyond reprehensible. But this man in front of him, this Uncle Sewell, dressed like Himmler, or Rommel, or Goebbels (he could never tell the Nazis apart), in a dull walnut suit, wearing Lennon-specs he no doubt felt made him look smart, *intellectual*, as Blake's father would have put it, *he'd* been the bigger demon. He'd molested his own niece. He'd violated her in unmentionable ways, turned her into a drunken basket case. Uncle Sewell represented all the men in the world who *ruined* women. All the men who lied, who cheated, who abused, who drove women crazy, inspired women to take out their frustrations on men who had the nerve to treat them with respect. Blake's fingers turned cold. His heart settled. He said, "Uncle Sewell?"

The man sniffled and wiped his nose with his naked ring finger. His tone of voice resembled a twelve-year-old's offering a snotty *So?* "Who are you?" His face scrunched like an irate infant, communicated annoyance at the notion he shared the Earth with a human being as low as Blake Ness.

Blake whipped out the gun and stepped forward. He squeezed the trigger without aiming. The pop pierced his eardrums. The kick jarred his hand. The side of Uncle Sewell's face chipped off like a piece of poorly sliced cake. Blake pointed the gun at the seeping hole in the man's jaw, between jagged, broken teeth, and fired again. Bone and blood and cartilage spat backward, decorating Blake's faded, navy and gold windbreaker. The man stumbled into his house. Both eyes remained intact, wide, horrified. Blake brought the gun to the center of the man's disfigured skull and fired two slugs into his brain. The repeated blasts tuned out birds and crickets and dogs barking louder with each shot, replaced them with a ringing, reminding him of hearing loss he'd experienced for days after attending heavy metal concerts as a preteen. Uncle Sewell collapsed. No movement, no spasms.

He'd read the resulting guilt of such an action could haunt a man. But it didn't. Uncle Sewell had earned his fate. Shortly before Blake broke up with the woman from New Orleans, she'd suggested he displayed traits of a sociopath, said she found vampires sexy and that, no doubt, explained her attraction to him. He'd apologized, assured her his bizarre love for Chelsea Farmer could not be cured, not even by a good woman like her. And that's when she'd reminded him he knew too much about her and promised to kill him.

Blake moved through the crowd of forty and fifty-somethings toward the bar, looking for a seat. The people parted for him, offering confused expressions, unable to figure out for themselves what compelled them to get out of his way. He felt no malice, he just refused to look down when any of the men huffed their chests, challenged him. He found a stool by the cash register and returned his attention, momentarily, to the television, to Linda Lee, now relating the shocking story of two lesbians claiming they'd been denied service at a popular fried chicken joint. Linda Lee suggested the CEO of the chain restaurant should be replaced. The parrot near the TV said, *Shame, shame! Shame on him!*

A younger man in a white Oxford and khakis approached from behind the bar. He spoke in a South American accent. "Good evening, sir."

"Don't call me sir," said Blake. "I don't sign your paycheck."

"Very good, sir," said the bartender. "And what would you like?"

"Been a stretch since I've had any booze." He studied the faded labels on bottles lining a shelf beneath the mounted television. "Better start mellow. Jack and Coke."

"Very good, sir." The bartender turned to fix the drink.

The parrot said, *Good, good, sir. Very good, sir.*

The bartender said, "Hush, Jane."

Sweet Jane, said the parrot. *Sweet, sweet Jane.*

Scanning the few people seated further down, Blake settled his eyes on the crossed legs of a woman in a tight, turquoise one-piece skirt dotted with abstract seashell designs. The woman stared back, half a smirk loitering on her lips. She'd feathered her blonde hair. She might not have been aware 1987 ended thirty years ago.

The bartender slid a short, fat glass filled, mostly, with ice and soda and a hint of the good stuff. "Will you make a tab, sir, or pay now?"

Blake pulled out the wad of cash in his pocket, peeled off a ten and asked how much. The bartender told him seven dollars. Blake gave him the bill. "Keep the change, sir." He looked at the woman in seashells once more. He waited long enough for her to acknowledge his glance, then shifted his attention to the television. Linda Lee read a story about an epidemic on New York subways of something called "manspreading." Men and women near him argued about who had what right to do what and when…One more exchange with the woman in seashells and Blake would eliminate the space between them and introduce himself. As he prepared to peek her way again, he stopped. The people in the bar had turned toward the concrete arch and made way for a slender man who could not have been a day over ninety. His beige pants and sportscoat blended with his bronzed skin. Despite the absence of the sun, he wore large, square shades, the kind Blake normally saw on truckers. A cigarette in a gold and black holder dangled from the corner of his mouth. He cradled an empty brandy snifter in his left palm and used his other hand to greet people. A stocky man who kept his cargo shorts legal with peach-colored suspenders addressed the old man as Mozo.

The bartender nodded to Mozo and produced a bottle of Hennessey. He weaved around the bar and chased him down to serve him.

Blake rotated just enough to catch the eye of the woman in seashells once more. She sipped from a straw jammed in a half-full margarita glass. Before he could stand and work his way to her, a wiry man in a short-sleeved, Persian blue coverall with a stitched, oval nametag, a man barely more than a skeleton, jumped in his face and spoke in a fly-away, effeminate Southern accent. "You stepping on private property?"

A sparse collection of tattoos dotted the man's arms. Some numbers. Something written in Chinese, or maybe Japanese. Probably a word like 'strength,' alerting anyone capable of reading it they were dealing with a tough guy. Blake peered over the man's bony shoulder, at the woman, then turned to the man and said, "Didn't see any signs saying I shouldn't."

The man froze, his eyes darting left and right. He opened his mouth to speak, then retreated to a snarl. He must not have been a detective, must not have surmised his chances in a rumble with a man unafraid to kill. He drew back to throw a punch. Blake landed an open palm on the center of the man's face. His nose leaked like a busted faucet, forcing him to stagger backward. The people who witnessed it gasped and those alerted by the gasps shrieked. The man's hands were soaked with his blood. The woman in seashells grabbed a stack of napkins from the bar and patted down her lover's face. She threw Blake an angry glare. Like it had been his fault her man had opted to test him.

The bartender rushed over. "Sir," he said, "they will call the police. They will say it is assault."

"Nope." Blake sat down and continued drinking his whiskey and soda.

"Excuse me?" said the bartender. "Excuse me, sir, but perhaps you should leave."

Sweet Jane, the parrot, said, *"Leave sir, leave. Perhaps you should leave."*

The bartender stumbled away from the bar and helped the woman in seashells escort her boyfriend to the bathroom under the concrete arch. The other customers fashioned a wide sea between Blake and them, gawking at him the way an audience in a court feigns outrage at a suspected mass murderer. Weak, uncreative, manipulated, controlled. *Sheep.* No different than the slaughtered animal on the beach. First staked to the ground, then offered up as a sacrifice to something greater, something unwilling to bend to the fabricated will of manners, the mirage of civility.

Good for them. Blake downed the rest of his drink. "Does this mean I'm not getting laid tonight?"

"*Nope, nope,*" said the parrot. "*Not getting laid tonight.*"

A rickety hand landed on Blake's shoulder. He gleaned no ill intent as the ancient celebrity Mozo sat next to him. "Well, my friend, it is as if you have walked in off the dusty streets of Laredo. The new sheriff in town, so to speak." He raised his brandy snifter for a toast.

Blake clinked his glass, rattling lonely ice cubes. "He asked me to dance. I obliged."

"That much is obvious." The old man extended his hand. "Mozo," he said. "I am the mayor of this island."

"You going to tell me to get out of town by sundown?"

"Nope." The mayor of Raro Key sipped his brandy.

Three

Mozo not only served as mayor of Raro Key, he owned it. He'd bought the land in increments after fleeing Cuba in 1959. In 1995, he purchased the last lot from an heir to the Disney fortune. Raro Key provided a haven for misfits who'd somehow found their way to the Florida Suncoast. Developers loitered on the island, nagged him to sell, offered, he claimed, astronomical sums of money. "Why would I?" he said to Blake. "I worked my life to secure this. It is mine. Nobody will take it while I breathe." He let it slip, at one point, that he'd been born in 1930. His parents had a potato farm in Cuba and raised him to believe labor led to reward. When the communists seized the government, Mozo joined the resistance. He snuck onto a cargo boat for Florida when it became obvious too many had been brainwashed by Castro. "There comes a time when a man must understand: his view of the world is too different from his neighbors. It is not the obligation of the neighbors to move on. It is the obligation of the individual to find his own tribe or, if necessary, create a new tribe." He swept his arm across the pre-dinosaurs in the bar and said, "These are my people. The office workers who retreat here at night to drink away the misery of their servitude." Then he pointed to the beach, to the hippies and the drummers. "And the lost and wandering youth, whom I love dearly, as though they were my own children."

A Sarasota County sheriff arrived. He spoke with the tough guy and the woman in seashells, both of whom cowered near hard, plastic picnic tables beneath the concrete arch. They pointed at Blake and the sheriff patted the tough guy on his shoulder and waddled to the bar. A gut resembling a butterball turkey loped over the sheriff's utility belt and beige pants. If Blake had decided to run, he doubted the man could keep up. Mozo stood and shook hands with him.

"Carter," he said to the sheriff, "what a waste of your time this is."

The sheriff waved a flabby thumb at Blake. "Folks tell me this here fellow's been-a throwing haymakers."

Mozo patted the stool next to him and suggested the sheriff have a drink.

"Not tonight, mayor," said the sheriff. "We need to square this here situation."

Blake started to speak. Mozo stopped him. He used his chin to nod in the direction of the tough guy and the woman in seashells. "Wallace made the disturbance, not my friend here." He held up his hand, pointed to his palm. "My friend did not close his fist. I have observed the entire conflict and I am satisfied there is no legal action necessary or even possible."

"Wally's wiping catsup off his face. How's an open palm going to do that?"

"Carter," said Mozo, "you have ever heard me tell a lie?"

The sheriff put his hands on his hips and attempted to stare down Blake. Blake returned the scrutiny. "All right, mayor. I'm a take your word for it." The sheriff started back toward Wallace and the woman in seashells, shaking his head, knocking loose whatever excuse he'd use to explain why the violent maniac at the bar wouldn't spend time in the bucket.

Mozo said, "Do not worry about Wallace. He is an employee of mine. I will speak with him in the morning, remind him to keep his cool around strangers. He is, as you have encountered, enthusiastic for conflict. A product of having never experienced a *real* conflict. Many of your people, forgive me for putting it in such terms, have had things too good to appreciate the danger of conflict."

Blake said he understood.

The mayor continued, "I look at you, my friend, and I see a man who is running. May I suggest Raro Key might be a good environment to slow you down, allow you to breathe, enjoy your life?"

"Last place I settled," said Blake, "just kicked up another dust storm, you know what I mean? I don't think I'm meant to stay put very long."

Mozo smiled. "We are soul brothers, my friend, I can already tell. Sixty years ago, I am just like you. I am wandering. But Raro Key, it seems like heaven, no?"

Nodding, Blake said, "It's a little too hot for my blood, but I did get the impression, out there on the beach, that a man could enjoy himself around here."

"Ah, yes." Mozo tapped the bar, motioned for the bartender to fill his snifter. "You are looking at the women, yes?"

"Yes, sir." He asked about the drums, the alligator.

"Wallace retrieves a sheep from my farm near North Port every night and the children of the beach, they carry out the ritual, appease Lalo's appetite so he does not feed on human flesh, a bad habit he developed early on that we have hopefully diminished if not completely eliminated."

"Lalo?"

"I may own Raro Key, but the earth, it belongs to Lalo."

The bartender asked whether Blake wanted more to drink.

"Actually," he said to both the bartender and Mozo, "I could use the name of a motel. Preferably one that'll take cash."

"There is no motel on Raro Key," said Mozo. "There are residential accommodations across the street, above the stores. Or, you are free to sleep on the beach."

"With that alligator running around?"

"The children of the beach, they sleep there every night without incident."

The bartender attended to customers at the other end of the bar.

"My friend," said Mozo, "I have an opportunity for you. The man who protected my girls at Let's Chill has recently moved on."

"The massage parlor?"

"Let's Chill is a legitimate establishment," said Mozo. "The girls, well, *yes*, they work in bikinis, because, as you see, this is a beach. The air can feel like the interior of an incinerator for the majority of the year. The women should be comfortable. This is my opinion. The men, the clients at Let's Chill, though, they do not always understand. Just because they are seeing the skin of a beautiful woman, this is not an excuse to touch her in an inappropriate manner. I have enough people trying to take this island away from me. These men who cannot control themselves, they could have the massage parlor shut down and bring unwanted attention. On such occasions as the men's hands wander where they should not, I need someone like you to convince the gentlemen to reconsider their behavior. On rare occasions, you will need to be more persuasive."

Blake shook his head. "I appreciate your confidence in my powers of persuasion, Mr. Mozo..."

"Please, only Mozo." He stretched his arms behind his back. "I have an idea. We will go to Let's Chill. You look haggard. You look like you could use an hour with, oh, who is working tonight?" His eyes crawled the straw roof for a moment. "I believe an hour with Emilia will do you some good. You may think about my offer in the meantime." He tapped the bar twice and stood. "Let us go, my friend. Midnight approaches."

The lobby of the massage parlor should have created no doubt in the minds of clients that they'd stepped into a business on the square side of the law. In addition to diagrams of the human body taped to cobalt blue walls above a plastic bench, two signs posted on the window in front of the receptionist's desk indicated requests for sexual services would result in swift removal from the premises. The air had been seasoned with lemon grass incense. Ukulele and Hawaiian steel guitar meandered from mounted stereo speakers. Mozo rang a buzzer attached to the window in front of the receptionist's desk and a woman in Spankees and a black tank-top rushed out from a dark corridor. Her wrinkled, stressed lips relaxed when she saw Mozo. "Oh," she said. "Good evening, sir."

"Good evening, Chelo." He put his hand on Blake's shoulder. "My friend requires attention. Emilia is working tonight, yes?"

The woman nodded. "She's with a client now. Should be ready in five to ten."

"Tell her to take her time," said Mozo.

Chelo swept her raven hair from her eyes and instructed Blake to follow her down the corridor. Plain, tiny Christmas bulbs strung along the baseboards wove a scant carpet of light. Long, Persian rugs covered the hardwood floors, muffled their steps. The sounds of a woman chopping a man's back with her hands traveled through one of twelve doors leading to private rooms. Chelo adjusted her shorts, as though she suspected Blake of ogling her, and opened a door at the far end of the hallway. "Just because Mozo says the service is comped, Emilia will expect a tip."

"I understand," he said.

She stepped aside for him. "Emilia will be with you in a moment." She pointed to a pair of plaid boxers on the massage table in the center of the room. "Slip those on." She started to leave, then stopped. "Mozo told you, no funny stuff, right?"

He assured her he'd seen both signs in the lobby as well as the one in the room hanging over a slim rack with oils and white towels. After the woman left, Blake stripped his clothes and put on the plaid boxers. He hoped to God they'd been properly washed. A degenerate he'd known in New Orleans, a football bookie named Dixon who weighed more than Blake's shitty Renault Encore, had complained of getting crabs in a massage parlor in Texas. Blake draped his clothes over a wooden folding chair angled by an opaque window. He settled onto the table, nestling his head inside the face cradle, adjusting his position so breathing wouldn't be an issue. His body melted into the foam padding. He had not realized how tired he'd become during the last hour. The room swayed with the hula music. His mind drifted, forced him to consider the woman he'd left in New Orleans:

Felicia Hill. Two years older. About a foot shorter. She'd run a motel in Metairie owned by her Uncle Theo. She wanted to buy it from him but couldn't muster legitimate funds. He allowed her to pay him by pulling hits, snuffing dealers and/or junkies who owed him money. Blake had lived in the motel for more than a month when she asked him where he'd come from, where he planned on going. He had no answers. This must have designated him a lost puppy, or however women referred to aimless men. He'd lied to her, told her he'd fled Kentucky. The one thing he'd been honest about: He had no idea where he'd wind up next. Felicia often worked the graveyard shift because she could find no one else to sit at the front desk from ten to six in the morning. Sometimes, she'd disappear in the wee hours and return with a blood stain on her clothes. She always looked troubled, as though she felt remorse. Blake pretended not to notice. He couldn't understand why she cared about her victims. Night after night, trading war stories of life in crumbling American cities, watching old movies on TCM in the motel's lobby, they talked themselves into sleeping together. The sequence of events unfolded the way Blake imagined normal romance flowered when he'd endured puberty, decades earlier. He'd spent the years in between trying to "figure out" women. Then he discovered, in middle age, he only ever needed to figure out himself. Robbing, killing, and, for a moment, pimping, had revealed his true nature—comfortable scoundrel. Society had not rewarded him for working a thankless, blue-collar job. That special bank of privilege television pundits and myopic college professors insisted he benefited from had never granted him any withdrawals. His descent into a life on the run felt much more like an ascent to *exactly* where he needed to be; this marked the beginning of his transformation into a confident man. In time, he moved in with Felicia, chipping in on rent for her apartment. She convinced him to attend church with her. He found the services lively, not so different from rock concerts he'd witnessed as a teenager. In bed, she read to him from her favorite philosophy books—Camus's *The Stranger*, Sartre's *Being and Nothingness*, etc. When he asked her how she reconciled her love of existentialism with her belief in God, she said, "You need to cover your bases." He'd suspected, then, he'd found the perfect woman. The only glitch: He could not stop thinking about women from his past—Chelsea Farmer and Lita Fisher, a woman he'd obsessed over in his twenties, a woman whose rejection he'd never overcome. According to Felicia, he often spoke their names in his sleep.

The door to the private room opened. Pink Lemonade, a scent strippers and prostitutes often wore, wafted through the air, seeped into Blake's nostrils. He said, "Hello." Memories of his previous life escorted the perfume across his senses. He hadn't had many professionals, but the girls he had paid, they always smelled the same.

In a soft, cautious voice, nearly a whisper, a young woman said, "I am Emilia. They say you requested me."

"Mozo suggested we have a session. I think he thinks you'll convince me to work for him."

"You will take Connell's job? You will keep the pendejos in line?"

Blake brought his arms up and rested his hands near his head. "I've been driving two days straight," he said. "My mid and lower back could use a workout."

Emilia dragged the chair with Blake's clothes on it across the floor, placed it next to the table. Without asking, she organized his clothes and rested them on an empty metal shelf. She stepped onto the chair and dug her toes into a space between notches on his lower spine. He could hear her struggle to grab hold of bars suspended from the ceiling. She balanced herself and inched her way up and down his back. She wedged her big toe deeper and deeper into his flesh. He grunted several times before she said, "Too rough?"

"No, no," he said. "Just getting used to it." He inhaled when she tasked his sore, aging muscles, and exhaled when she released. The wave of steel guitar from the speakers soon joined the dance.

The woman worked Blake's calves and returned to the floor. She sprinkled oil on her hands and rubbed from his ankles to *just* inside the boxers he'd been provided. Her fingers grazed his thighs. He cleared his throat, tried to distract his libido with memories of his fourth-grade teacher smacking his knuckles for failing to write pretty, cursive letters. Emilia made her way up his arms and stood at the front of the table, kneading his shoulders. Blake lifted his head and lost a breath gazing directly into the woman's pastel bikini bottom, her smooth, tanned legs. Before his rational mind could stop him, he reached forward and grabbed her. She stepped away far enough for Blake to glance up at her, take in her straight, black hair, her emerald, cat-angled eyes. She said, "Please, sir."

No wonder they needed a bouncer. Blake looked at the young woman again and turned up his palms. "I apologize." The woman folded her arms. The worn expression on her face suggested she went through this constantly. Blake said, "All apologies, really." He put his hands on the table, dipped his head into the face cradle and relaxed. As the woman finished the massage, he thought of the line between himself and Uncle Sewell. How he wanted that line to be a wall, a wall surrounded by a moat, a moat surrounded by a ravine. He decided, thus, to accept Mozo's offer. The mayor promised a room, rent-free. The minor salary would pad his nest egg, his smidgeon of power in the world. The woman told him to sit up. She instructed him to put his arms behind his head as she stretched his spine left and right. She slapped his back with the bottoms of her fists.

"Finished." The woman climbed off the table and placed her feet in aqua blue flip-flops she'd left by the door.

Blake reached into his pants, pulled out two twenties and thanked her.

Mozo met him in the lobby, asked if he'd enjoyed the massage. Blake told him he'd take the job for a little while, see how things went. He did not reveal that sooner or later Felicia Hill would find him and put a slug between his eyes. Mozo led him to his new apartment, located above the massage parlor. They climbed the stairs of an iron fire escape attached to the backside of the building. Blake's knees protested. He ignored them, feared such pain signaled old age, mortality. The mayor told him others lived on the second floor, so he should keep noise to a minimum.

The door to his room had no lock. "Do not think about this," said Mozo. "Raro Key is a safe place, as the children like to say." The walls of the room had been painted a shade of blue darker than the massage parlor. No kitchen, just a mattress on springs that squeaked like a small animal fearing its life, a pea-green dresser with a transistor radio on top of it, and a cramped bathroom. Mozo said he'd pay him two-hundred a week, under the table, with which Blake could feed himself. He wished him a good night. "The girls," he said, "they are tired of fending for themselves when they are trying only to work." He said they'd come get him if they needed him. Blake hoped the women handled their randy customers the way Emilia had dealt with him. He intended to spend most of his time on the beach, breathing clean air and meeting available women.

He retrieved a ratty, navy and gold gym bag containing clothes and a toothbrush from the hatchback of his Renault. He carried it under one arm and cradled the shoebox of money underneath his other. He loaded his socks, boxers, T-shirts, and three pairs of pants into the top drawer of the dresser. Unzipping the gym bag's side pocket, he pulled out his Smith & Wesson .38, the revolver he'd used to kill Uncle Sewell. Before murdering the pedophile, he'd dubbed it *Crystal*, the nickname Chelsea Farmer used when she'd allowed him to pimp her out to perverts. He doubted he'd ever see the young woman again, inform her he'd been the triggerman who'd put her uncle in the morgue. He placed the gun behind his socks, assuming he wouldn't be wearing them too often on the island. Then he set the shoebox in the lowest drawer. If Mozo had lied about the island being safe, about the lack of a lock on his door being nothing to fret over, he'd deal with the old man the same as he had Wallace, the tough guy with the woman in seashells.

Before turning out the lights, he tuned the transistor radio on the dresser until he found a lone signal, a station playing Big Band from World War II. The music took him to the town of Haggard, Indiana, near Gary. His grandparents had a small house on Lake Arthur. He'd visit them every Christmas. His grandfather, who'd fought in the Pacific, played crackling Benny Goodman LPs on a turntable built into a cabinet with an embedded black and white television. Must have been state-of-the-art in 1959. His grandfather had taught political science at Indiana University Northwest, in Gary. He described the tides of influence in the United States and the rest of the world with one word: Power. Before his grandpa died at the turn of the century, he had a final conversation with him about Bill Clinton. His grandfather had been a conservative for some time and, while considering Clinton intelligent, could not fathom how a man in such a position could risk it all for a moment's pleasure with a twenty-two-year-old. Having been in his early twenties, Blake didn't understand it either. In his late thirties, however, he would be tested the very same way by Chelsea Farmer. And he failed. Miserably. His grandfather, apparently, did not respect the influence Clinton's intern possessed. If he had been alive then, Blake would have told him, "Power wears many masks."

On the street below, illuminated by the storefront windows, a lone panther strutted down the middle of the road. The tawny brown, muscular cat turned its head left and right, not so much like a hunter, more like a mother seeking something she'd misplaced. The panther trotted on and disappeared in the darkness. Blake wondered if he might need to carry Crystal, his .38, at all times. Alligators? Panthers? What else roamed free on the island? He lay on the top sheet on the bed, unsure of what condition the mattress might look should he remove the sheet and investigate.

Underneath the warm, nostalgic music, a groaning settled in the air. It sounded as though something heavy had been hung from wooden beams running overhead and it had taken to swinging back and forth, a rhythm conjuring images of a fantasy world where Blake Ness had done as his parents had urged—he'd studied, gone to college to become an expert in complaining about America, and taken a faculty job, as his father had, and married, and had children, and someday, in the future, attended a party with his devoted wife, and they danced on a hardwood floor, swaying, like the stress on the beams in his room, to Glenn Miller's "In A Sentimental Mood," and he looked into his imaginary wife's eyes and realized familiarity had left them no choice but to love each other in a manner rendering their eventual deaths much, much more painful than necessary. Another reason to believe in something beyond life, something greater than mortality. Something to make the pain worthwhile.

Four

After his morning stretching and exercises, Blake washed himself in the tub in his bathroom, an old-fashioned number lifted off the floor with brass feet resembling dragon claws. He finished showering before the water turned a decent temperature. No towels available. The window frames cracked like knuckles as he let in natural air. People passed on the thin sidewalk below. If they looked up, he waved. The moment they realized they were ogling a naked, middle-aged man, their eyes raced for the ground. Some shook their heads, as though a man unashamed of his body warranted inclusion in debates over the definition of purest evil.

Satisfied his clothes wouldn't stick to him, he slipped into boxers, socks, pants, and a faded, blue and white Jim Harbaugh jersey. He traipsed down the steps on the backside of the building and ducked into the diner on the opposite end of the block. Abstract paintings of various species of birds, Blake assumed exotic, local birds he'd never see in the Midwest, hung at different levels on the dandelion-colored walls. The scent of fried food beckoned from a pass-through over a stainless steel shelf. Five sherbet-orange booths lined the window, stolen perhaps from an abandoned Howard Johnson's. Alternating ruby and black vinyl cushions covered the spinning stools at the counter. A few leaked cotton stuffing like wounds from a knife fight. He greeted a couple he figured close to his age. Their husky frames stretched the fabric of their designer safari shorts and button-down shirts. Their dirt-smudged faces suggested they'd slept on the beach. They ignored him when he asked, "Rough night?" He spun the stools, testing their wobble-ratios, and chose a seat at the farthest end of the counter. A woman in her sixties clomped out from behind the grill, a pad in her hand and a striped tarantula lounging on her shoulder. The waitress retrieved a pencil from behind her ear. Her dark, slick hair had been pulled into a ponytail and wrapped in a hairnet. Blake could smell her cigarette habit as she approached. She introduced herself as Koko, tugging on a plastic nametag pinned to the apron covering her bubblegum pink uniform.

She said, "What you need, hon?"

Blake asked what she recommended.

"House special," she said. "Fried egg. Piece of lettuce. Served up on two pieces of toast. Wonder bread, you know, because wheat bread'll clog your shitter. Pickles on the side. You can eat those separate or put them on the sandwich yourself. I like them on the sandwich. I think it helps things move in the morning, you know, on the toilet. But, to each his, her, or their own, you know?" Then she spoke in a hushed voice, as though telling a dirty joke. "We prefer freedom of choice around here."

"That sounds fine." He'd have to find a grocery store and figure out a way to prepare meals for himself. "Large glass of orange juice'll do good, as well."

"Sure, hon." Koko wrote the order on her pad and slid it across the steel counter under the pass-through. She asked if Blake wanted coffee while he waited. "Just made it five minutes ago."

"No thanks." He'd had booze the night before, an all-American toxin he didn't often put in his body. No need to further the damage with caffeine.

"Suit yourself." She poured herself a cup and set it down near him, as though it might tempt him to change his mind. She fished a lighter and a pack of Kool cigarettes from a pocket on her apron. She lit one and ashed in a sink near the pass-through. She took care to exhale away from the spider on her shoulder. "You don't look like our usual customer, you don't mind my saying."

The yuppie couple, in unison, coughed. The man said, "We're trying to eat here, Koko." He held a paper napkin in front of his mouth, not quite covering his TV cop-style mustache.

She blew smoke in their direction. "You know where you are. You don't like it, drift on over to Venice, where they put up with highfalutin schmucks like you."

The yuppie woman spoke through her fingers. "Really, Koko? *Really*? All the money we spend here?"

"You drop a few dimes in the summertime. Big deal." Koko tapped her cigarette over the sink. She turned her attention back to Blake. "You were saying, hon?"

"I didn't say anything, ma'am."

"Call me Koko."

"Sure thing."

"You know who you remind me of?"

Blake tried to hold his breath, protect his lungs without being obvious.

"Second-hand smoke's a conspiracy," said Koko. "Somebody in the tobacco industry pissed off someone royal. Maybe one of those Soros brothers, or whatever those rich pricks are called, maybe someone they actually gave a shit about cashed themselves in with Marlboros. You know how it is—one person gets hurt, the rest of us got to pay."

He shrugged. "Maybe."

"No maybe about it," she said. "This country was built on tobacco. All the sudden, we're going to pretend we didn't know this shit is harmful? You're taking fire into your lungs, people. What genius couldn't see the problem a hundred years ago? Except, they didn't move to ban the shit a hundred years ago. They started in on cigarettes in the early 90s. You old enough to remember?"

"Thank you, ma'am..." Blake raised his hand to stop her from correcting him. "Koko. My fault. Thank you, *Koko*. And to answer your question, I was supposed to be in college in the early 90s."

"What happened?"

"Guess I wasn't smart enough."

She laughed and choked. "All you need to get into college is some daddy issues and a writing utensil." The spider on her shoulder stirred. She stroked it with the same hand cradling the cigarette. "Settle down, Pearly May."

"Maybe you're right."

The cook smacked a classroom desk bell on the shelf under the pass-through and slid a plate with Blake's food across it along with a squat glass of orange juice. Koko rested her cigarette on the edge of the sink. She did not wash her hands before carrying the order to Blake. She set the plate down and nearly dropped the glass, spilling enough to make him wonder if he should ask for a replacement. His stomach protested, having eaten nothing but a veggie sandwich over the previous twenty-four hours.

Koko said, "*Any*-hoo, you know who you remind me of?"

"I sure don't." He slipped the two slim pickles on the side of the plate in between the bread and the egg. He took a bite. Pretty good. Grilled to a crisp. Enough salt to sire a thousand heart attacks. He thought of meals he'd made for himself when he still schlepped for a living—ravioli from a can, spaghetti from a can, tomato soup from a can. Nothing but additives and the illusion of satisfaction.

"You ever see that flick, about a taxi driver? Bobby Pacino, or whatever his name is…guy goes bonkers over a blonde, takes her to a porno theater, she's too uptight to enjoy it, she dumps him, he tries to assassinate a filthy politician, screws that up, decides to shoot a bunch of gangsters instead? Like, he's in love with this thirteen year old or something. Weird movie."

"*Taxi Driver?*"

She flashed a grimace at the spider on her shoulder. After taking an epic drag off her cigarette, she said, "Stupid name for a flick." She ran water over her cigarette and dropped it into the sink. "Not that I think you're bonkers, hon. That mole under your right eye, looks like the mole on Pacino's face. That his name, Pacino?"

"I think that's somebody else."

"Some Hollywood weirdo, thinks selling violence to the masses is a good idea." The waitress inhaled three more cigarettes, going on about movies and television and conspiracy theories. Blake got the sense she might be flirting. When new customers entered the joint, she snuffed her last smoke and attended to a quartet of hippies who, like the yuppies, looked as though they'd spent the night on the beach. Blake paid his tab, left Koko a five-dollar tip.

Before heading back to his apartment, he stopped off at the

record store. It didn't open for another hour. He moseyed down the sidewalk and started for the backside of the building, hoping to change into something more appropriate for the beach. Several men in suits, each carrying clipboards under their arms, stood in the parking lot across the street, pointing toward the swamp, Lalo's kingdom. Blake marveled at their ability to wear that much fabric in the Florida heat without passing out. A young woman in a coconut bra and grass skirt rushed from the massage parlor. Her short hair flapped like tiny wings as she hustled up to Blake and asked his name.

"Chelo needs your help." She tugged the sleeve on his shirt and ran back inside.

He kicked at several broken seashells on the sidewalk before following her.

"What took you so long?" Chelo stepped from behind the reception counter.

A man in one of the private rooms huffed and puffed—"You're going to give me a refund, so help me, I'll sick the law on this place so fast your heads'll spin."

"Where is he?" said Blake.

Chelo pointed to a door halfway down the hall, on the left. "Number four." She mumbled as Blake passed her, "Why is it always number four?"

The door had been left open a hair's width. Blake pushed it further and entered. A pear-shaped man covered in enough body hair to earn him a spot on an evolution chart, a towel wrapped around his lower body, circled the massage table, fists clenched. His face had flushed from all his shouting. A young woman with wild, greasy blonde hair, dressed in a sleek, black bikini bottom and neon-green top had wedged herself in an uncluttered corner. The man's gray suit pants and jacket had been draped over the back of a wooden folding chair near the door. His polished wingtips poked from beneath the massage table. He'd probably read an ad for the parlor in the back of a local independent newspaper and assumed Let's Chill was just another rub-and-tug. When he saw Blake, he stopped.

"The hell are you?"

"Listen, bubba," said Blake, "signs on the walls are serious."

"I put down sixty bucks," he said. "This bitch doesn't pull it till it spits, I want a refund. How difficult is that for you bums to figure out?"

"Did you get a massage?"

"What's that got to do…"

Blake repeated his question.

"Yeah, so?"

"Tip the girl and hit the road."

Phlegm dribbled from the man's lips. "*Tip her*? Are you insane?"

Blake nodded toward the woman in the corner. "Don't you hear the bones in their hands begging for mercy when they knead your bloated belly? This ain't easy work, bubba."

"You some kind of white knight?" The man squinted, approached Blake with his head craned. "One of these male feminists thinking you'll get some, you just kiss enough female ass?"

"I belong to no tribe," said Blake. "Now, I'm going to ask you, politely, to leave, one more time. I play two-strike baseball, you dig?"

"I got an idea," said the man. "How about you take your two-strike baseball and shove it up your ass?"

Blake grabbed the man's ear and pulled him into the hallway. The man slapped at his hand, clawed it, kicked at his shins. Blake said, "Eight pounds of pressure, bubba. That's all I need to rip your ear off the side of your head." As they approached the door to the lobby, Blake shouted to the woman in number four, "Bring his fancy clothes!"

Chelo and two more women in white, frilly bikinis looking no different than panties and bras stood in the lobby. They glared at the large man as though he'd thrown up on them. Blake said to Chelo, "You got his money?"

She nodded.

"All right, then." He used his foot to shove the door open and sent the man tumbling over the sidewalk and into the road. The woman from number four threw the man's clothes at him and flung his wingtips across the street. They landed on one of the entrances to the parking lot. Before the man could stand, an SUV crushed them. He smacked the pavement and cussed. He glared at Blake with the same look rich people always produced when the world didn't spin their way—*How dare the tides of the universe defy me?*

"You try to come back here," said Blake, "I'll kick the dog shit out of you."

"I know people," the man said as he stood. "I could have you killed."

"Promises, promises." Blake closed the door.

Five women, including Chelo and the woman from number four, stood in the lobby. Chelo thanked him. "We get those all the time."

That last sentence didn't register with him. Not right then. "Should I just hang out here?"

"No, no," she said. "Clients see a man in the lobby, they turn around and leave. Connell, he used to chill at the diner. Made things easier for all of us."

"And you're open seven days a week?"

She grinned. "Eight in the morning to midnight."

A young woman wearing a flesh-colored, one-piece bathing suit said, "You like reading?"

"Nope." Blake turned to leave.

"If I were you," said Chelo, "I'd find a simple hobby."

Five

Blake shot the shit with Koko for half an hour. The massage girls called on him again, this time to smash a wooden chair across the face of a bodybuilder who believed the woman in a black bikini bottom owed him a blowjob. "Her fingernails grazed my balls," said the meathead. "If that's not a promise, I don't know what is."

Blake told him he should feel lucky any woman would touch him anywhere. The meathead swung wide. Blake grabbed the back of the wooden chair and heaved it with both hands, splintering it against his skull. The chair cracked and the meathead dropped to the floor. Blake nudged him with his foot. "Still breathing." He told Chelo to call an ambulance.

"Nah," she said. "They drop like this, Mozo wants them taken to lockup." She used her cell phone to contact the sheriff and a white van arrived ten minutes later. Two deputy sheriffs cuffed the slumbering meathead and carried him to the wagon.

The younger of the two, crew-cut, clean-shaven, said, "You working Connell's old job?" Something wicked laced his tone, like maybe he'd been good buddies with Connell and resented Blake taking his place.

"Seems so."

The other deputy said, "Good luck." He'd given up on basic hygiene, let his hair grow into a mop his ears poked from like children peering through hedges.

Back and forth. Right up to midnight. Blake met every waitress and cook who worked at Deep Fried Heaven. He yapped with tourists, yuppies, hippies, and yippies. Gave in to the need to stay alert with caffeine. Men, it appeared, could not read. They did not understand the word 'no.' If the women in the massage parlor slapped them in their faces, they interpreted the violence as foreplay. They resented Blake explaining to them how, even in a massage parlor, women, not men, determined what happened to their bodies. The dumbest clients who, for whatever reason, tended to come off as the richest, had the most difficult time falling in line. "You wouldn't want someone pawing at you if you weren't interested," he'd tell them. "What makes you think it's any different for her?" By the end of his first day on the job, his arms were exhausted from throwing punches and dragging the belligerent ones through the hallway and out into the street. When midnight arrived, he slumped to his room and collapsed on the bed. He didn't even have the strength to tune the transistor radio on the dresser. Staring at the ceiling in the dark, he noticed shadows shifting in sync with the groaning wooden beams. Half asleep, he dismissed what appeared to be the profile of a human being, hanging from the rafters. As he closed his eyes, he heard a voice say, *Mind yourself around here*. It seemed to come from his father. He had no idea where either of his parents were, if they were even alive. When they intruded upon his dreams, they remained the age they'd been when he left his father's house at eighteen. He had now reached that age himself and had nothing significant to show for his near-half a century on the planet. He awoke several times that night, panicked by the notion he might die and leave no trace of his existence.

He would learn the truth of Connell Riggins the next day. During a morning recess from dragging horny, disgruntled customers from the massage parlor and either sending them on their way or helping deputies load them into paddy wagons, he listened to Koko delineate the history of crack cocaine in the United States. "First case," she said, "first recorded case of someone dying from smoking too much crack? Happened on a boat coming here from the Bahamas, or some shit like that. 1979, 1980, somewhere around then. South America? Late 1970s? What do you think of?"

Blake said, "I don't."

"*Jonestown*. You think of Jonestown." Koko lit a cigarette and exhaled in his face. "You paying attention? Jonestown. Think about it: How does a goofy white boy from Indiana control so many black people? Politicians go there to check it out, see something they don't like, *boom*. Gunned down at the airstrip. Next day, everybody in the camp is dead. Kool-aid, they told us. Bullshit. How come over half those folks had bullet holes in their backs? Because they were trying to flee."

"I've never heard any of this," he said to her. "Where'd you get this? Television? The Internet? Not a damn thing on the Internet you should ever take seriously."

"I *know* this shit, hon," she said. "I put it together myself. Crack shows up in the hood right after Jonestown. You know about the boxcars in South Central?"

He said he did not.

"Oh, shit, hon." She ashed her cigarette in the sink and asked if he needed a refill on his coffee. As she poured, she said, "Little kids, playing in the ballpark, you know? They see this train car on abandoned tracks. Just shows up, out of the blue. Where the hell did it come from? They investigate, open it up. What's inside? Stacks of unregistered guns. Crack arrives around the same time. *Boom*. Street gangs go from beating each other up over looking at each other's women to shooting each other in the face for slanging shit on the wrong block. You think that was an accident?"

"Toughest thing in the world to accept is coincidence."

"Bullshit," she said. "For instance, you know what happened to your predecessor, right?"

"Excuse me?"

"Riggins, Connell Riggins, the big bad sonofabitch who did your job before you."

"Not a clue." He wished one of the women from the massage parlor would rush in and retrieve him.

"You never met a man more jolly, more at odds with his occupation. Big fellow, let me tell you. Filled the doorway. Giant beard, like a beehive, dangling off his chin. Dye it white, he could be Santa Claus. Used to see him on the beach, at the drum circle, dancing with the youngsters, smile on his face you could spot from outer space."

"Wait a minute," said Blake. "How the hell did he have time to go to the beach?"

"Oh, don't worry, hon," said Koko. "Once you establish a reputation, word'll get out. The perverts'll stop getting so grabby with the girls."

That had been a spot of good news, a moment he felt he could take a breath and relax.

Then Koko said, "So, back to Connell Riggins. Suits from Dolent Enterprises, some real estate outfit, they started sniffing around here, next thing you know, the happiest man on the planet ties a rope around his throat and hangs himself."

Coffee raced down the wrong pipe and Blake choked. "*What?*"

She tossed him a mildew coated towel and continued: "Real fancy pants, these Dolent fellows, up and down the block. Mozo finally had Connell tell them to skedaddle. They start pushing back, so Connell calls the sheriff's office. Two deputies show up, take one look at these monkeys in suits, get back in their cruisers and leave. Connell shows these Dolent boys just how tough he could get, picks one of them up and lands him across his knee. Other fellows had to carry the poor sonofabitch back to their BMW. I asked Connell what the hell was going on, he says these guys talk in funny accents, like they're from across the Atlantic."

"European?"

"Farther than that," she said. "Sounded Russian to Connell."

"Maybe the Russian mob?"

"Maybe. Except, I asked Mozo, he said they were from Belgium. Connell, bless his heart, not the brightest lamp on the block, you know what I mean?"

Blake asked how long ago that had happened.

"Two weeks, hon." Koko stroked the back of the tarantula on her shoulder. She cooed to the spider, "Is Pearly May hungry? Yes, she is. Yes, she is."

Tiring of the waitress's conspiracy theories, Blake left the diner. He started for his apartment, then stopped, thinking about the traces of whatever nastiness had nabbed Connell Riggins, lurking in his room like a ghost. Not that he believed in such things. Like heaven, ghosts eased the fears of the living. A simple equation: If ghosts existed, something happened after death. Life's toils possessed meaning. He turned himself around and visited the other businesses on the block. The mysterious store in the center, Trascendente, contained nothing more than empty shelves and a wooden counter with a circle carved in its center. The walls had been painted a shade of yellow lighter than the diner. A woman in her sixties or early seventies, based on her pure, white hair wrapped in a neat bun over the gray, thin skin covering her skull, sat behind the counter. She greeted him.

"Hello," he said.

"Not seen you before."

"Mozo hired me the day before yesterday."

"You must be the new muscle." She offered a nervous, fragile hand. "You must be Connell's replacement."

As he grasped her fingers, feeling her bones beneath soft, loose flesh, he read the nametag pinned to a manila blouse a few sizes too big for her: Ginger. "I'm Blake," he said. "Just checking out the neighborhood."

She reached under the wooden counter she sat at and produced a small, velvet sack sealed with a golden thread. She opened it and three dice spilled out. She placed them in the center of the circle on the counter and said, "Roll."

"Excuse me?"

"Pick up the dice and roll them."

To humor the woman, he did as instructed. He shook the dice and let them drop onto the counter. One bounced off the edge and onto the floor. Ginger shook her head. "That's bad news." She stared at the die on the floor, frowned. "Bad, bad news."

Blake wished, once more, one of the girls from the parlor would shout his name.

"You should expect trouble. Very soon." Ginger pointed her nose toward the runaway die. "But let's attend to the number you've produced." She tapped the dice left in the circle. "Two sixes. Not bad. Six plus six, as you may know, equals twelve."

He laughed. "They still taught basic math when I went to grade school."

"A twelve means you will be contacted soon about something very important."

"Any idea on what?"

"The dice only reveal the outline, not the details."

He started to leave.

She said, "Have you noticed anything unusual about Raro Key?"

"I've seen an alligator the size of a Buick demolish a sheep."

"That would be Lalo, yes."

"At night, a panther casually walking down the road."

"Ah, yes," she said. "That would be the ghost of Marabella. She is waiting for Mozo to join her in the next world."

"She's…what?"

"Mozo's lover. A married woman. Her husband had her killed when he realized his daughter shared none of his genetic information. The daughter's identity is a secret to most, though it is rumored Mozo has included her name in his will."

"I see." Blake reached for the door.

"Watch out for the wolves."

"Wolves?"

"Definitely not indigenous."

He passed the diner, waved to Koko, who appeared to be offering coffee to her spider, and entered Vinyl Destination. The odor of stale cardboard and records set upon him as the door squeaked shut behind him. 1950s Mambo cooled the air with machine-gun congas and Celia Cruz's sweet, muted voice. It came from a record playing on a sky-blue, vintage suitcase player propped up on a wooden Tillar pedestal. Whoever owned the joint didn't believe in climate control. The insane heat outdoors barely dissipated in the muggy store. Rows of boxes containing original pressings sat on top of two tables pushed together in the center. Against the far wall, more crates had been lined up on wobbly, plastic tables. Along the wall closest to the front door, a long, glass display case supported a cash register and a row of turntable needles. A dozen records filled the inside of the case. Several Beatles albums, the covers of which he'd never seen before, dominated the pricey selection. Blake approached the counter and peered over it. A woman squatted on the other side. Her denim shorts had inched a bit lower than she might have preferred in public. She turned around, glared at him. She held several coins in her hand. They looked as though they'd been gathering dust for decades.

"Treasure hunting." She had dark skin, long, wavy hair, and round eyes reminding Blake of the woman from New Orleans. Or Chelsea Farmer. Or Lita Fisher. Or any other woman who'd ever crawled under his skin and left a mark. "What can I do you for?"

"Just taking a stroll through the neighborhood."

"You the new Connell?"

"How's that?"

"Friend of mine from the art school in Sarasota said he tried to get one of the girls to give him a tuggy. Said you showed up and scared the shit out of him."

"Just doing what I was hired to do."

"I got no problem with you keeping the place copacetic." She opened the cash register and distributed the dirty coins into the appropriate trays. "My friend's a douche-nozzle. I told him Connell had, you know, passed on, and first thing this guy does is cross the bridge to pay for a handjob. What a dork."

"Well," said Blake, "lot of massage parlors in the world offer exactly what he wanted. This just happens to be one that doesn't."

She turned a smidge sideways and studied him. "Whole thing is stupid, you ask me. What kind of man needs to pay for it? Plenty of horny women out there."

"Some men don't understand that."

She asked him his name and told him to call her Mina.

"Like Mena Suvari?" he said.

"Who's that?"

"Don't worry about it."

"Cool. About lunch time. What say you hang out with me at the diner?" She locked the drawer on the cash register and stepped around the counter. Her flip-flops sounded like a child snapping bubblegum for attention. As she passed Blake, a mature scent greeted him.

"Fendi?"

She blushed. "I know, it's for old ladies. But I like it. Smells like something mystical." She locked the door as they exited and grabbed her shoulders. "A little chilly today."

"It must be a hundred degrees."

"Can't be more than ninety."

Before they entered the diner, Eunice, a woman from the massage parlor, stepped onto the sidewalk. As the door to Let's Chill closed, the sound of a man with a high-pitched, anxious voice trailed into the humid air. Eunice, no taller than five feet, hustled over on high heels. She'd worn a green, sparkly one-piece skirt that hiked with each step, revealing her army green panties. Despite skin paler than fresh snow, she spoke wanna-be hip-hop with a southern twang. "Yo, Mr. Ness! We got a situation."

"Dammit," he said.

Mina joined him as he made his way to the massage parlor. A slender man in gray khaki pants and a sky-blue and white-striped button-down shirt bounced on his feet, a closed Bible in his raised hand. His blond hair had been quaffed like a character from a 1950s *Archie* comic. His chameleon eyes bulged and wandered in opposite directions. Before Blake entered the building, Mina grabbed his arm and said, "Connell dealt with this prick, just days…"

He thanked her and allowed Eunice to duck inside ahead of him.

The man with the Bible assessed the newest member of his audience. "Well, well," he said. "What have we here? Sodom to the Gomorrah these harlots peddle?"

Chelo angled around the man and stood next to Blake. "This clown," she pointed at the bug-eyed man with her chin.

"I'm stepping on ground fashioned from the loins of the Creator," said the man. "I am violating no laws. I cannot say the same for you whores." He nodded at a group of women huddled by the door to the hallway. "Surely you ladies understand why opening your legs for profit is an abomination to all that is good and pure."

"Nothing illegal goes on here, bubba." Blake moved closer, anticipating the necessary tactics to overpower the man and throw him out, should he fail to cooperate.

The man scoffed. "Is that a sick, twisted joke? Look at these whores…" His arm waved in the direction of the women. "You think they're dressed for *work*?"

"They are," said Blake. "Their attire is entirely appropriate considering the amount of sweat they produce and the fact that we're in Florida, a goddamn oven."

Clutching his Bible with both hands, aiming the cover at Blake, the man said, "He who protects sinners shall perish with them."

"Where's it say that?"

"Well," said the man, "it's implied."

"You've taken enough time from everyone here." Blake opened the door. "You can leave on your own, or I'll assist you."

The man brought his Bible back to his chest and clutched it like a mother protecting an infant. "I refuse."

Blake snagged the man by his collar and dragged him toward the street. The man brought his arms back and crashed the Bible into Blake's face. The strength with which he administered the thwack didn't match the shock Blake felt when the book's soft leather binding smacked him in the temple. He slammed an open palm into the man's chin and launched him through the air. The Bible flipped and landed at the feet of the women huddled by the corridor. Eunice had joined them. She kicked the book across the floor, at the head of its owner.

"You must not know who I am." The man inched to his feet. He picked up his Bible along the way, dusted it off. He scowled at the women. "How dare you harlots touch this. How dare you."

Blake hurled him out the door. The man struggled to keep his balance. "I don't give a good goddamn who you are," said Blake. "I see you on these premises again, I'll beat you within an inch of your life." The man screeched as Blake closed the door on him. His chameleon eyes threatened to leap from his skull and bounce down the sidewalk. Blake turned to the women and said, "Let's give him a chance to be on his way."

A pair of college boys in white slacks and matching golf shirts with Greek letters stitched into them showed up and knocked on the glass. "Hey bruh," said the one tapping on the door, trying to hoist his voice over the sound of the Bible thumper. "Sign says you're open."

Blake poked his head out. "Come back in about fifteen minutes. Women need some time to get ready."

"Bruh," said the other kid, "this is totally uncool."

"I hear you, ah, *bruh*." Blake did his best to smile, to look like he gave a shit. "Do yourselves a favor, head on down to Deep Fried Heaven and grab yourselves a malt."

The kid who'd knocked on the window wrapped his fingers around his buddy's sleeve. "Bruh says the women need time? Let's give the women time." He didn't lower the volume of his voice as he composed an a-rhythmic strut down the sidewalk and said, "Probably got to powder the puss, bruh." He punched his buddy in the shoulder. Psychobabblers on TV would no doubt read Freudian nonsense into the gesture. Blake dismissed them as idiots. He figured he'd be called right back to the parlor to evict one or both of them. The man with the Bible produced a smartphone and snapped a picture of him. Blake shot from the parlor, tried to grab the phone from him, but the man with the Bible ran off.

Blake said to Chelo, "That guy's been here before?"

She nodded. "Two, three weeks ago. Connell gave him the boot. The bastard said Connell would pay. I guess it upset Connell enough." She stopped herself, maybe wondering whether Blake knew the fate of his predecessor. "Well, you see Connell is no longer here."

"Yeah, I picked up on that." He returned to Deep Fried Heaven. In the diner, Mina pushed an empty plate away from her. Blake said, "Mind if I sit down?"

"I have to get back to the store," she said. "Maybe we can meet for dinner. I prefer to eat at the bar, on the beach. They make decent Hawaiian barbecue."

"Jesus, I didn't know there was more than one option around here."

"Yeah, greasy pork gets tired after a while." She clasped her hand over her mouth and glanced at the counter. The staff appeared to be in the kitchen. She relaxed. "How about six-thirty? Give me time to close up and make sure I don't look like I've been working in a sweatshop."

"You look fine."

She left a tip on the table and stood. "Later." As she turned to leave, she stopped and leaned close to Blake. "Don't take this the wrong way, but this is just social."

"Sure thing, boss."

"You work for Mozo. Not me."

Blake watched her leave, watched her hips twitch in that calculated manner the gods invented to prevent men from ever achieving total control over their gonads. He stayed in the diner and, against his better judgment, drank coffee for the remainder of the afternoon. The women from the massage parlor did not call on him again. The sun dripped into the western sky. He payed his tab and retreated to his apartment to gather some more cash in case… what? Mina, a woman he barely knew, agreed to go on a midnight cruise with him down to the Keys? He imagined making love to her on a beach as night blended into day. A fabricated image he'd probably seen in a *Hustler* magazine somewhere in the 1980s. He opened the bottom drawer of the dresser in his room and stopped, backed up, and looked around for signs of unwanted visitors.

His shoebox full of money had been taken. A slip of paper had been left on the side of the drawer the shoebox previously occupied. He picked it up and turned it over. In different, pasted-on letters, similar to a ransom note, someone had written:

We know who you are

Six

Whoever had broken into Blake's apartment had not taken the time (or cared) to find Crystal. He retrieved the .38 from under his boxers and socks, checked the cylinder to make sure the intruders weren't playing a trick, leaving the weapon with no bullets. The gun remained loaded. He stuffed it into the front of his pants and headed for the beach. The drum circle pounded with a special ferocity. The tribe of youngsters had grown since the night he'd pulled into town. Perhaps the weekend had arrived. Mina waited for him at a wicker table in Lonesome Cowboy Bill's. She'd changed into a frilly blouse and cream-colored skirt. She waved to him. He nodded and scanned the bar for Mozo. He pulled out a bamboo folding chair opposite Mina.

She said, "Trouble?"

"Nothing to fret over."

"You look like Connell did, the day he threw Bible Boy out of Let's Chill."

The drumming swelled. Blake's attention wandered to the crowd gathered around the torches. The staked sheep's bleating sounded like a hysterical vocal, not quite in sync with the percussion instruments. He thought of a world music festival he'd attended with Lita Fisher in the early 90s. A host of rich musicians, mostly British, carting out indigenous, so-called Third World acts like museum artifacts. The crowd, rich kids high on weed and mushrooms and acid, obediently applauded, turning to each other and gushing. As though the idea of music existing in non-Western countries was too miraculous to behold. The alligator stomped out of the darkness and put a swift end to the sheep's ballad. The kids dancing among the torches backed into a clump, blocking Blake's view. He said to Mina, "Did Connell talk to you before he croaked?"

"Ouch," she said. "That's not the kindest way to put it."

"The man's dead," said Blake. "I doubt we can hurt his feelings."

"Connell didn't say much." She traced her pinky around the rim of a tall glass of beer. "In fact, he pretty much clammed up after that. Kept to himself."

"I see." Blake asked if she'd ordered.

She showed him the menu, a one-page, laminated card with barbecue and a selection of sauces and nothing else. "You trust me?"

"Until you give me a reason not to."

"Cool." She ordered at the bar.

The middle-aged drunks parted and Mozo, now accompanied by a woman maybe one-third his age, wove through the people to a table near Blake's. He offered the woman a chair. She'd decided a purple bikini top and thong appropriate evening wear. She'd paid for, or maybe been gifted, a set of bolts bigger than her skull. Blake wondered if she'd been imported from Miami. He scooted across the sandy, concrete floor. "Hey there," he said to Mozo.

The old man didn't look upset by the intrusion. "I hear you are doing outstanding work at Let's Chill."

"This guy gives massages?" The woman spoke at a helium pitch.

"Please, Teresa," Mozo said to the woman, "we are discussing business."

"I got a problem," said Blake.

Mozo put his arm around Blake's shoulder. "Please, tell me. There is nothing we cannot fix on Raro Key."

"Somebody lifted something personal from my apartment."

"When did this happen?"

"This afternoon."

Mozo placed the fingers on his free hand in a crevice between the boards composing the tabletop and ran them back and forth.

"Let me ask you this: Did you have a disagreement with a man claiming to be holy?"

Blake nodded.

"Listen to me, my friend, you must watch yourself. These events, they took place several weeks ago. Things did not end well for the man who did this job before you."

"So I've been told."

"There are vultures everywhere in Florida," said Mozo. "Not all of them have wings. Whoever this man works for, they are very powerful. My suspicion? He is with Dolent Enterprises. They have been trying to swindle me out of my land for some time now. They want to make Raro Key like every other cookie-cutter resort beach in Sarasota. They frightened the man who did your job before you, frightened him enough to convince him to take his own life."

Blake would have preferred to throttle him, ask him why the hell he put him in this situation. Mozo's date, drenched in Pink Lemonade, briefly distracted him. He looked back at him, realized the old man had achieved existential overtime and deserved to do whatever he wanted. He said, "I may have to leave."

"I would not hurry so, if I were you." He snapped his fingers at the bartender, held up his brandy snifter and tapped it. "Connell Riggins, he is the man who did this job before you. He was a good man. A very good man." He nodded his chin at Mina, who, Blake realized, had been giving him a dirty look. Mozo continued, "The record lady, your companion there, she adored him. Connell was as big as a bear, the bears you see in mountains, the kind you never want to meet when you are walking in nature. His heart? Ten times bigger." He demonstrated with his hands, putting them together and pulling them far apart. "I adore this man very much, but he is, ultimately, a giant pussy cat. You, my friend, you have *the look*. We share this, you and I." Now, he whispered—"You have actually taken a human life."

Blake tried to laugh.

"Do not deny this, my friend." Mozo produced a cigar from the breast pocket of his shirt. "It is written all over your face. You possess the stare of a man who has killed and walked away, unscarred by the hypocritical legal machines fooling our lesser brothers and sisters into believing we are a civilized species. I murdered many in Cuba. With each bullet I put into the beating heart of another, my skin became thicker. This cannot be seen by others, as you know. It is something you experience in the mind." He tapped the side of his head.

Looking back at Mina, Blake signaled he'd be right over. He said to Mozo, "Things get too nasty, I'm checking out. In the meantime, I'm going to figure out who broke into my room and I'm going to treat them to a torture technique involving pliers a piece of shit cop once showed me."

"For this, I do not blame you." Mozo raised his glass again. He shouted at the bartender, "Hector, why do I wait so long?"

On the television, Linda Lee, dressed in a low-cut, blazing-red blouse, read a report about a protest at the art college in Sarasota. The picture switched to a montage of images of people dressed in black throwing trash cans at a Starbucks and a First American bank. One of the hoodlums denounced the latest soundbite from the current president. The rotund young woman spoke through a bandana covering her face. "It's like he's *literally* Hitler."

Sweet Jane, perched to the side of the television, flapped its wings and squawked, *Hitler! Hitler! Literally Hitler!*

Blake returned to the table with Mina. A waiter in a sky-blue and white Hawaiian shirt, a lei made of plastic orchids around his neck, brought two steaming platters of meat, potatoes, and sliced pineapples to their table. "You need anything else, let Hector know."

"You tell Mozo about Bible Boy?" Mina said to Blake.

"Sort of."

"Son of a bitch." She dug into her food, gobbled a fork-load of pork. "He just sat by, let them get to Connell like that. Now he's going to do it to you."

"I thought Connell killed himself."

"That's the official story." She took three monster bites.

Blake tried the pork. He complimented the woman on her dinner suggestion. Then he said, "Everyone on this island a conspiracy theorist?"

She stopped chewing. She swallowed and grabbed a paper napkin from a metal dispenser in the middle of the table. "Connell would never have taken his own life. The only time he ever seemed depressed was right before the end, right after he dealt with Bible Boy."

"Did he tell you why?"

"He refused to spend time with me. Said it was for my own good."

"He was scared?"

She looked down and continued eating.

They didn't speak of Bible Boy or Connell Riggins for the rest of the meal. Out on the beach, the hippies split into small clusters engaged in orgiastic activities. Bodies relieved of clothing heaved in piles. He pointed with his fork over Mina's shoulder. "Gratitude," she said. "To Lalo. For eating the sheep and not them."

"That's legal? Right there, in public?"

She shrugged. "Raro Key's not really beholden to the rules uptight folks on land adhere to."

In the end, he paid for the dinner. She revealed she lived down the hall from him. He walked her back to her apartment. Just before she nudged her door open, he stepped closer. She placed her painted nails on his chest and pushed him away. "I told you, I'm not interested in getting involved with anybody. Especially Connell's replacement."

"I understand." The door swung shut with a soft click. Upon returning to his place, he said, "Am I the only person on this island who can't get laid?" He checked everything twice, made sure he hadn't been robbed again. He flipped on the transistor radio. "Sentimental Journey" filled the room with a gnarled melody. He inspected the bottom drawer of the dresser, hoping he'd hallucinated the absence of his money. The note informing him the thieves knew his true identity remained. He wondered just how in the hell he'd track down the money. Couldn't go to the cops and complain about cash he'd stolen from someone else. After tucking Crystal in the drawer with his socks and underwear, he turned off the light and stripped down to his boxers. A Big Band version of "Claire de Lune," one he'd never heard before, smoothed out the wrinkles in the atmosphere. As he walked toward the bed, he caught the shadow of a man, hanging by the neck, swaying across the floor in rhythm with the music. The beams in the ceiling creaked. He said, "I don't believe in ghosts."

A baritone voice answered, "Good for you." Blake told it to shut up. The ghost said, "No can do, buddy."

Blake sat on the edge of the bed. He rested his head in his hands. "Jesus Christ," he said. "I can't afford to go insane. Not right now."

"You can't afford anything. Not right now."

"Get lost, bubba."

"Don't you want to know who took your money?"

He opened his eyes. The shadow of the dead man no longer haunted the floor. "No, that's okay. I've floated under society's radar for two years thanks to that stash…."

"Now, is that sarcasm, or cynicism? I could never tell the difference."

"My dad would have called it being a smart ass."

"Mine too."

Blake crossed his legs and spoke to the blue and yellow night. "Why'd you kill yourself?"

"No choice."

"Mina must have dug you something fierce."

"The feeling's mutual, trust me."

"I think she thinks, I don't know… She's like Koko, a conspiracy theorist."

"Conspiracy theory is just a term the masses rely on to avoid confronting who's really sticking that grand phallus up their keisters. The moment somebody utters something that's actually true, people surrounding him will slap a label on him, like, say, 'paranoid,' they'll say, 'Oh, Bob? He thinks international corporations run the world. He's just *paranoid.*' They'll shuffle him off to a head doctor who will either have him committed or fill him up with psychotropic drugs, depending on how stubborn the doctor thinks Bob's addiction to the truth is."

"*You* sound paranoid, if we're being partial to the truth."

"I know better." For a moment, the shadow on the floor returned. The impression of the man in the noose raised its arm and tugged on the rope tied around his neck. "Believe me, I know better. And if I'm to believe the men who stole your money, you should know better as well."

And then the ghost said Blake Ness's real name.

"That man doesn't exist anymore," said Blake.

"To you, maybe. To the control freaks with real power in this world, you're whoever they need you to be."

Power.

His grandfather's word for the tides of influence.

The stairs outside squealed under the weight of at least two people. They clomped down the hallway. Light from the corridor fractured as they stood at Blake's door. He started for the drawer with his gun in it. A pair of men as tall as the doorframe entered the room. The second man hit the light switch. Blake shielded his eyes to protect them from the sudden glare. Both visitors wore Hawaiian shirts speckled with pineapple designs, khaki shorts, and sandals. Aside from their height and attire, they had little, physically, in common. Like Laurel and Hardy—one slim, probably ate his vegetables when his mother told him to, the other, chunky as an adult pig, just before the slaughter.

"Put some clothes on." The skinny man jammed his pinky in his ear, dug out a nugget of wax, sniffed it, and flicked it against the wall.

Blake remained seated on the bed.

The other man clapped his hands, two meaty paws as big as oven gloves. "We ain't got all night."

"You chumps take my money?" Blake stood. An idiotic gesture, considering the round guy could knock him out with one punch.

The skinny man, possibly the cerebral half of the operation, said, "We took the cash. But we're not the ones who have it."

The other man said, "You were told to put some clothes on."

Blake approached the top drawer of the dresser.

"Make a move for that revolver," said the skinny man. "It'll be the dumbest thing you ever did with your life. And from what I gather, you've set some world records for dumb."

"And here I thought you two were the champs."

The other man smacked him in the back of his head. "Talking smart like that might fly with the loonies on Raro Key. It don't sell so well with the mainstream." He pointed at a pile of Blake's clothes on the floor. "We ain't asking a fourth time."

Seven

Blake christened the men Tweedle-Dee and Tweedle-Dum. At least for the ride through the humid night, across the bridge, into Sarasota. Tweedle-Dee, the skinny man, the one possibly possessing a two-digit IQ, sat in the passenger seat. His partner, Tweedle-Dum, drove, both hands on the steering wheel, his ogre frame leaning toward the dash, like he could barely see out the windshield. Tweedle-Dee tuned the radio in the SUV to a pop station. An uninspiring mix of hip-hop and dance music polluted the air. Tweedle-Dum bobbed his head. He'd been blessed with goon stature, a firearm, and a job with somebody who believed gangsters still held sway beyond Hollywood movies. He'd bully his way through life until either a cop snuffed him or misery eased a bullet from his own pistol into his gumdrop brain.

The dummy directed the SUV along the coast. North, it seemed. He turned onto a dirt road and slowed at a gate in front of a draw bridge with wooden slats. Tweedle-Dee stepped out and punched the numbers 1-9-9-5 onto a keypad posted to the side of the bridge. The gate opened, Tweedle-Dee got back in, and they proceeded across, the wheels of the SUV thump-thump-thumping over the slats like the drummers on Raro Key. On the other side, the wheels settled on a dirt road watched over by arching willow trees. Tweedle-Dum tapped a knob jutting from the steering column and the SUV's brights cast a pale glare into the fog rising off the ocean. Insects darted in front of the vehicle, some not surviving the challenge. In the distance, a manmade construction blotted out a half-moon. As they got closer, the shape revealed itself to be a mansion resembling a small, European castle. Towers with pointed roofs bordered the exterior. Candlelight illuminated the windows. Tweedle-Dum pulled into a roundabout in front of what appeared to be the castle's main entrance and parked. Tweedle-Dee turned and said, "Do yourself a favor: when talking with Mr. Stinson, don't ask too many questions. He gets all killy when people come off more inquisitive than he'd prefer."

"That the mistake Connell Riggins made?"

Tweedle-Dum slapped the steering wheel.

"You see?" said Tweedle-Dee. "Even my brother here is allergic to curiosity."

Ah, brothers. That explained their shared, bulbous nostrils and the stupid dents at the tops of their noses, like God reached in and swiped a nugget of gray matter. Blake opened the door for himself and stepped out of the SUV. Aside from a thin skirt of dried mud along the bottom of the vehicle, its gold exterior sparkled in the electric moonlight.

The goon brothers led him into the castle. Esoteric symbols decorated the tiled floor—triangles with eyes inside, swastikas, runes similar to the symbols on the Led Zeppelin record with the Levee song. The sort of oddball scribbling compelling legitimate conspiracy theorists to shit their pants for the last five hundred years. They passed massive, wooden doors, all shut. Mono-rhythmic dance music emanated from the basement. They climbed a set of winding, stone steps. Slim windows shaped like upside down crosses allowed a view outside. The castle had been built on the edge of the land. Mediocre waves slapped the shore below. He followed the goon brothers through a red door at the top of the staircase.

On a patio, or balcony, Blake couldn't be sure what the official term for it might be, Bible Boy sat at an oval table next to an elfish geezer in giant, square glasses. His snow white hair, fashioned like a 1970s talk show host, matched his horseshoe mustache. He burst into a smile when he saw Blake. He rushed to his feet and rounded the table. "What a pleasure, what a pleasure!" He shook Blake's hand without waiting for him to agree. "Sit, sit." Metal scraped against the brick floor of the balcony as he dragged a cast iron chair from under the table.

Blake obliged, waiting for the right moment to toss the little man over the side of the tower.

The man returned to his seat and said, "I trust William and Billy here were good to you."

"I thought they were brothers."

"Oh, yes. Twins, twins," said the man. "Delightful. Absolutely delightful, don't you agree?"

"William…and Billy?"

The goon brothers grunted. No doubt they'd tired of such questions long ago.

"Don't ask," said the old man. "Their mother didn't know two were on the way. Named the first William. So overwhelmed when the second arrived, she called him Billy. Yes, Billy. Only real crime being, if William ever wanted to be called by the natural, shortened form of his name, he only had Will to choose from."

"I hate the name Will," said Tweedle-Dee.

"That's neither here nor there." The man tapped the table with three fingers. "You've met Ethan." He nodded to his right, to Bible Boy.

"Ethan?"

"Ethan Hammond. Like the organ." He glanced at Bible Boy and giggled.

"Ethan's a nuisance," said Blake. "And he gives religious people a bad name."

Bible Boy leaned forward.

The old man said, "Oh, that's just a little act we put on. Brings out Mozo's hired muscle."

"So, in addition to being a jackass, he's a liar?"

"You're calling *me* a liar?" said Ethan. "Pot, meet kettle, don't you think?"

"I think I should have broken your neck when I had the chance."

The goon brothers chuckled.

"Now, now," the old man put his arm out. "We're having a friendly chat. Friendly, friendly, yes?" He introduced himself, "I'm Don Stinson. Perhaps you've heard of me."

"Nope."

"Well, your mayor there, on Raro Key? He's a bit of a dictator, you ask me. Not so different from the fascist in the White House."

"It's his island. He can do what he wants."

Ethan waved his hand left and right. "Tomato, tomata."

"No matter, no matter," said Don Stinson. "I want someone else in charge of Raro Key."

"Buy him out," said Blake. "Looks to me like you got the means. Moneywise, that is. That's how things get done in this world, right? Money?"

"Sometimes." Don Stinson nodded to Ethan, who stood and walked through a blue door on the opposite side of the balcony. "In the case of Mozo, things are different. He's built a sort of cult on that island and everybody, even the residents of Sarasota, go right along with the illusion that the island's not being wasted on a bunch of freeloaders. That's quality real estate begging to make some shiny nickels."

Blake leaned back in his chair.

The blue door opened, and Ethan returned with Blake's shoebox under his arm. He placed it on the table and said, "About two-hundred thousand."

"Two-fifty." Blake folded his hands into fists.

"Your math skills are questionable," said Don Stinson. "My boy here wouldn't skim." He passed a parental glance Ethan's way. "If he says it's two-hundred, it's two-hundred. That's all beside the point." He stood and clasped his hands behind his back. "The only way to eliminate Mozo is, well, to eliminate him."

"That's where you come in," said Ethan.

Blake shook his head.

Don Stinson said, "Are you familiar with your predecessor? Connell Riggins?"

"Heard of him, sure."

"He no longer walks among us."

"Well…shucks."

"I'd like to go about this business a bit different this time." Don Stinson returned to his seat. "The money you stole, it belonged to an organization bigger than anybody here."

Sweat gathered in the crevices of Blake's palms.

"Look, you and I, we have something important in common." He waited for Blake to show interest. "We're Hoosiers. We're bound by the land we were born on. I just happened to luck out. I was born in a wealthy family, connected, and you, well, you were born to middle-class losers who believed they were making a difference. Losers, indeed. You saw through that, didn't mess around with going to college, listening to senile, geriatric leftists spew nonsense, and then attempting to tote those expensive bullshitting skills to an unsympathetic job market. Good for you, by the way. Good, good, good for you. No, you were just one of the unfortunate masses, dragging your head close to the ground, like Charlie Brown, for goodness' sake, until you saw an opportunity to take a slice of power that didn't belong to you." The smile on his face grew. Light rising from the many windows in the castle revealed Don Stinson's eyes were pitch black. They bugged a bit, like Ethan's, and, despite the influence he must have had he looked, deep down, afraid for his life, like he'd made a bad decision at some point and felt he could never recover. "But, a word of advice, Lester Banks: You haven't gotten away with anything. Not a gosh darned thing."

Blake cleared his throat. The urge to deny his former identity begged to find sound and escape. He clenched his teeth. Contesting something untrue, in a world turned upside-down, only convinced accusers they were correct. And, who was he kidding? He had been Lester Banks. Once upon a time.

"I mean," said Don Stinson, "if it had been necessary to call on you before now, someone would have wrangled you sooner. Say, in New Orleans?" He raised his white eyebrows. "When you robbed Jerry Simon of his folding cash, when you busted into his bungalow in Hamilton County, you showed your face to a dozen different security cameras."

Determined not to speak, Blake blinked a second too long. He sighed. How could he have screwed up like that?

Don Stinson read his mind. "A man of Jerry Simon's stature hides his cameras in the walls, behind mirrors, paintings. Only those who don't know better put a camera right out where a thief can spot it. They believe this will deter criminals. A man as desperate as you obviously wouldn't give a rat's hairy tookus. Not one bit."

"This is an entertaining lecture." Blake pushed himself away from the table. "Unfortunately, I have to work in the morning." Tweedle-Dee and Tweedle-Dum lurked behind him.

"We'll get you to school on time," said Don Stinson. "But first, you need to know what you're going to do for me..."

"Jack shit." Blake rested his hands across his belly. "That's what I'm going to do for you, bubba. Jack shit. Have I repeated myself enough times?"

Mimicking Blake's positioning of his hands, Don Stinson said, "You haven't even heard what it is I want you to do."

"If what they say about Connell Riggins is true, it can't be good."

"Connell was a snowflake. My mistake was thinking he had what it takes to kill a man."

Blake studied the square, cobbled stones in the floor of the patio, the lines of dirt seeping through the cracks between them.

"You, on the other hand," said Ethan, "have murdered in cold blood. A one-man killing machine, yes sir." His addiction to clichés reminded Blake of a cousin of his, Jeffrey Sandal. He'd last seen Jeffrey at his wedding. He'd married a stripper named Greta. He hadn't spoken with him since childhood. Evidently, Jeffrey had grown into a non-stop cliché factory. And, like Jeffrey, Ethan delivered tired phrases without the slightest awareness.

Don Stinson stood once more, now taking on the appearance of a general overlooking a map before an invasion. "So far, Lester, you haven't claimed innocence of any of this."

"My name's Blake. There is no Lester Banks. Not anymore. You want me to take you seriously, you call me Blake. How the hell am I going to say I didn't take the money when it's right there, in front of you? As for this murder business..." He shrugged and looked away. A sure sign he'd laid the foundation for a lie.

"Sewell Harper," said Don Stinson. "I knew him from the clubs in Indy. Sewell's cameras were in the open, but, I guess, when you've decided to shoot somebody in the face with a cheap pistol, you're just not looking for these types of things."

"Uncle Sewell was a demon," said Blake. "A child molester."

Don Stinson's gleam returned. "Oh, Sewell Harper was a nasty son of a gun! Nasty, nasty, nasty. Little boys strangled and dropped in the White River over the last two decades? More than likely, Sewell's work. But, you're a citizen, you have no power, and at the time of Sewell's death, there's no evidence to suggest he represented any kind of threat to you."

"Yeah, well…" Blake stuffed his hands in his pockets. After some thought, he said, "All this evidence, why hasn't the law picked me up?"

Drawing in his face, Don Stinson said, "Surely you don't think we send the cops after somebody unless we *want* to? We just wait until we need someone like you to do something unpleasant, something we'd prefer not to do, for whatever reason." He nodded to the goon brothers. They rounded the table and disappeared behind the blue door for a moment. When they returned, Tweedle-Dee carried a long, black, plastic case under his arm. He set it in the middle of the table and opened it. Inside, a rather old-fashioned-looking rifle with a scope attached to it rested on dark, spongy padding. Don Stinson said, "You are to figure out a time when Mozo will be among people and cut him down."

Blake stood. "Mozo, as far as I know, isn't a goddamn toucher. You want to call the cops on me? Toss me in a cage for killing Uncle Sewell? Fine with me. Free room and board sounds great."

The goon brothers surrounded him.

"You'll get your money back," said Don Stinson. "You'll never be bothered again."

"Bullshit." Blake angled for the red door. "Soon as Mozo hits the dirt, cops'll be all over me."

"No, no, no." Don Stinson motioned for the goon brothers to give him room. "We've already got someone to take the fall. You're going to be a free man. You can take your stolen money and go anywhere you please. Anywhere at all."

Blake shook his head. "No can do, Mr. Stinson. Mozo's lived through some serious shit. He deserves to walk the Earth until gravity calls him home."

Ethan and Don Stinson blurted out dismissive, condescending laughter. "Okay, okay," said Don Stinson, "I guess you still don't understand how power works here. As in, who's got it, and who doesn't."

Blake headed for the red door. The goon brothers followed him. Tweedle-Dum turned him around. Don Stinson said, "Let's take a walk, ah, Blake, is it? Yes, yes, of course. I'll go along with this fantasy that Lester Banks no longer exists." He led the group to the blue door and through it. They descended another spiral staircase, this one without windows. The trip down seemed longer than the journey to the roof. The temperature decreased. For the first time, Blake felt underdressed in Florida. Mono-rhythmic thumping shook the walls as they neared the landing. Disco lights painted the floor with shifting, kaleidoscope colors. The stairs let out at a room the size of a basketball court. A crowd of men and women in suits, evening gowns, and Lone Ranger masks across their eyes observed a throng of nude teenagers heaving in a Bosch-like mass. They danced on a glass floor illuminated by an indigo glow. Each of them had been decorated with a tattoo of a black scorpion on their lower, right stomach, the stingers raised, arched, aimed at their belly buttons. As Don Stinson escorted Blake closer to the center of the room, the glass floor revealed itself a five-point star. At the top of the pentagram, a DJ dressed in a flower-pot hat, like a member of Devo in the "Whip It" video from the previous century, bobbed to the headache-inducing noise blasting from cabinet speakers set up on the other four points. The dancers appeared to be no older than fifteen or sixteen. Blake scrutinized the few who made eye contact. Their exaggerated, blood-red sclera suggested they'd been drugged. Don Stinson slapped Blake on his back. "What do you like, the gals? The guys?" He put his finger to his chin. "You defended the honor of a young woman, yes? Yes, of course. It's obvious. I'll assume you like girls. Once we demonstrate why you now work for us, you're free to take any of these morsels to a private room upstairs and do whatever your heart desires."

"Oh," said Blake, "I think I'd like to watch one of these kids cut your throat open and piss down your neck."

Don Stinson plowed through the bumping and grinding teenagers and called the DJ from his perch.

Blake stood on the glass floor. Something swarmed beneath it. Forcing sweaty, inebriated teens out of his way, he cleared a space to get a better look. Eight and nine-foot striped tiger sharks whipped at each other as they darted back and forth like dogs anticipating food. Don Stinson called over the goon brothers. They moved among the teenagers like predators. They closed in on a young woman with sky-blue hair. Her full breasts indicated she should have had pubic hair. But the pedophiles of the world, of course, demanded their prey resemble children. The DJ switched the music to something more urgent. The beat narrowed to one bass hit, over and over. He might as well have been playing a scratched record. The stoned teenagers must have interpreted this as a signal to boogie their way off the glass floor. The tiger sharks swam in a tight circle. A chain with a leather strap attached to the end lowered from the ceiling. Don Stinson joined Blake and said, "You'll want to take a step back."

The girl stared into the crowd with a grin on her face. She reminded Blake of footage he'd seen of the Manson family. Her vacant eyes confirmed she had no idea why she'd become the audience's focus of attention. The goon brothers lifted her and slipped her arms and legs into the leather strap and tightened it. Blake moved to stop them. Tweedle-Dum wrapped a paw around his face and shoved him toward Don Stinson. The old man poked his side with a stubby .22 cradled in his palm. "There are no heroes in this world," he said. "You know this. You *know* this." The goon brothers yanked on the chain. Whoever operated the harness lifted it so that the girl hovered, parallel to the floor, unable to protect herself if she should fall and crack the glass. Tweedle-Dee then produced a pocketknife and sliced intersecting lines into the girl's belly. She giggled as her blood drizzled downward. The goon brothers stepped off the rumbling dance floor. The partitioned glass separated, disappearing inside slots built into the foundation. The young woman's blood splashed into the water. The DJ isolated the beat—no bass, no synthesizer, just a repeating kick drum, like a mindless parrot:

Thump-thump-thump-thump-thump…

The well-dressed adults who had, until that moment, hidden in the shadows on the perimeter of the room, joined the crowd lining the pentagram. They clapped out of rhythm. As the harness lowered the girl into the water, the audience erupted into a unified howl, as though attempting to awaken beasts from another dimension. The sharks ripped the girl into pieces. Blake managed to look into her eyes, just before a fish obscured his view and tore into her skull. She did not seem scared, only confused as to how her short life had arrived at that final, brutal conclusion. The leather strap, now frayed and fractured, lifted from the water, covered in the girl's blood. The glass floor glided back into place and the adults in suits and dresses removed their fancy clothes and joined the teenagers as the music filled once more with bass and synthesizers and resumed its grating monotony.

Eight

Blake crept up the fire escape. He carried the black case containing the rifle by its handle. He'd been given forty-eight hours to accomplish his task. He put the rifle in the bottom drawer of his dresser, where his money should have been. When he turned the on/off dial on the transistor radio, nothing happened. He picked it up and tapped it twice. It had no cord attached to it. He removed the plastic guard in the back for the batteries. Empty. The ghost said, "Sorry, buddy." The radio switched on by itself. Frank Sinatra and Tommy Dorsey cooled the early morning air with "Imagination." Hints of the sun, approaching from the east, colored the slats on the windows' blinds. He twisted them shut, as tight as they'd go, and lay down on his bed. "So, they asked you to bump off Mozo," said the ghost.

"Not going to do it."

"I made the same decision."

"They told me they helped you with the noose and all."

"Oh, buddy, they were super friendly. Used the butt of a pistol to knock me out when I walked into the room. Before I know what's happening, they've got my neck in the rope, the rope tied to this here beam. Before I could protest, do anything, you know, there I am, just a-dangling away. Like a piñata, just swaying in the summer breeze."

"I've dealt with people like this before," said Blake.

"Not this level."

"What should I do?"

"Depends," said the ghost. "You one of these nihilists, doesn't believe life has any meaning? Disregard them until they turn out your lights. You got any attachment to things like breathing, I'd suggest you figure out a way to at least make it *look* like you did what they wanted."

As Blake's mind drifted into the sea of tranquility between consciousness and slumber, Felicia Hill, the woman from New Orleans, sporting a short, orange and white-striped dress he'd peeled off her many a wild night in Metairie, stepped on his chest, her platform high-heels digging into his rib cage. "You're in deep shit now," she said. Chelsea Farmer visited him next. She stood on beige sand, framed by an apricot sunset. She'd wrapped a thin, see-through fabric around her hips. A cherry red bikini top and a matching scrunchy bunching her undisciplined hair complemented her sheer skirt. She turned away from him and swayed toward the blinding sunlight. He tried to follow her, but another woman's voice whispered, "Not yet."

At breakfast, Koko chain-smoked and discussed 9/11 while Blake attempted to eat a fried egg sandwich. He stared at the food, rearranging it on his plate, as though that might make it more appetizing. Koko said, "I'm president on September-eleven, I ain't flying around the country like a coward, hiding from these so-called terrorists, no sir. I'm in front of television cameras, soon as that second plane hits the towers. I'm telling anybody who'll listen: Look, we think the son of a bitch responsible for this shit is hiding out in Afghanistan. If you live in Afghanistan, you got relatives in that shithole, tell them to pack a bag and hit the road. Twenty-four hours from now? *Boom!* Crater City."

"Pretty sure most of the people in Afghanistan had nothing to do with it." Blake removed the top of his sandwich and tried switching the positions of the pickles.

"Hell," said Koko, "they may have had *nothing* to do with it. May not have been Osama or any of his people. May have been the CIA. They drugged their own employees in the 1950s. Slipped LSD into their coffee without them knowing and observed their behavior. One poor fellow, he ended up under an overpass, holding his knees, shaking like he'd just met his savior. Any organization willing to torture their own like that, shoot, you can bet they won't give a shit about anybody else. I know they killed both them Kennedy brothers. Best believe they'd have no compunction sending a few thousand Americans to their deaths."

Blake removed the pickles. Tried to take a bite. Didn't taste right. "Here you go again, Koko. They're going to slap all sorts of labels on you."

"I'm comfortable with that, hon. This screwy society we got cooking, that's all they do. Offer up an opinion they don't like, they smear you. Doesn't matter which team you're rooting for—the elephants and the jackasses lost all concept of civil disagreement somewhere between the conman from New York in the White House and the shyster from Chicago before him."

"I don't think you're paranoid, Koko." Blake sipped his orange juice. Tasted like metal, or maybe blood. "I'm thinking, more and more, maybe coincidence isn't as common as we've been asked to believe."

She pointed her cigarette at him. "Now you're talking."

"Let me ask you something." Without waiting for her permission, he said, "You believe in sacrificing yourself for the greater good? You know what I'm saying? That shit Spock said in the *Star Trek* movie everybody likes, 'the needs of the many,' you remember that?"

Running her cigarette under water in the sink, she said, "Hon, don't ever let them fool you into giving up your life for some phony cause. I'd like to think we got further adventures on the other side of the grave, but I'll be damned if I've seen a hint of evidence that tells me we do anything but rot. Folks can call that selfish. That's okay. Just another smear. It's not selfish when they look out for themselves, no sir. Only when they've got someone else's life for currency do they get so compassionate and generous. You ask me, humans are animals. Animals are selfish. So be it. Why you ask?" She adjusted her hair under her hairnet. Didn't wash her hands afterward.

Blake pushed away his plate. "Just some thoughts keeping me awake at night." He placed cash on the counter.

Koko spoke to him as he left the diner. "Life's too short, hon. Look out for yourself."

He thanked her and headed down the sidewalk. In Trascendente, Ginger appeared to be organizing invisible items on the empty shelves. Blake ducked in and said, "Morning."

The old woman wore a burnt, salamander sundress dotted with yellow, sickle-moons. Her wooden jewelry rattled as she hurried back to the counter.

"I wondered," said Blake, "whether you might allow me another roll."

She retrieved the velvet bag and let the dice slip into her soft hands. She jumbled them a bit and placed them on the surface of the counter. "Give me a good one."

Blake cradled the dice and scattered them inside the circle.

Ginger touched her finger to her chin and clicked her tongue, as though she disapproved. "Bad news, lover."

Blake rested his palms on the counter.

"Snake eyes and a two," she said. "You can't find a more evil, unlucky number than four."

"Great."

She patted his hand before continuing. "Four is a harbinger of terrible things on the horizon. The good news about all dark ages, however, is that, eventually, they come to a close. What waits on the other side of the abyss can only be positive." She gathered her dice and returned them to the velvet bag. "Whatever path you're on, you cannot change it. You must follow through with whatever it is you've been asked to do. I suspect this has something to do with the massage parlor? Or maybe the businessmen I constantly see surveying the land? Look like they want to tear everything down and plant a golf course. That's usually what men like that do."

He shook his head. "I'm afraid this is a bit worse."

The old woman put the cloth bag under the counter. She tilted her head and smiled. "Quite a change since our last conversation, Mr...Ness, was it? "

* * *

Blake sat on the roof, waiting for sunset. Don Stinson instructed him to gun down Mozo in the evening, when the old man arrived at Lonesome Cowboy Bill's. Nicer cars full of couples or groups from the mainland pulled into the lot across the street. Mostly forty and fifty-year-olds. An occasional senior citizen. The hippies arrived by microbus or by foot. Young men and women dressed as though they'd recently worked on a *Mad Max* movie lugged drums of all sizes through the concrete arch. A pickup truck with a caged animal parked near the entrance. Wallace, the tough guy from the bar, now dressed in a navy coverall, opened the gate on the truck and led a sheep out of the cage and onto the asphalt. He walked the sheep to the beach and returned a few minutes later without it. The drumming commenced and the sun began its descent. Emilia, the woman who'd calmed his bones the night he'd arrived in Raro Key, roamed the sidewalk below, calling his name. He clanged down the steps and caught up with her.

"Mr. Ness?" she said.

He nodded.

"Some kid from Ringling. Thinks Amber owes him sex. Making a storm, he is."

Blake followed her into the parlor, to room number four. A young man with the sides of his head shaved and a moussed clump of hair on the top of his skull had tipped over the massage table and now sat in the corner tearing apart a *Sports Illustrated*. He crumpled each page and tossed them at a wire-meshed wastepaper basket near the door that had, for some reason, a small fire burning in it. "Bubba," said Blake, "we got a problem."

The kid surmised him with an ugly, pompous sneer. "You the janitor?"

Blake asked Chelo what she intended to do about the fire in the trashcan. She said she'd sent a girl to the diner for an extinguisher. "All right then," he said to the kid. "I guess word didn't get to your side of the tracks. This joint is for massages only. I'll give you one chance to leave on your own. You take it for granted, I'll drag you out of here by your stupid-ass Tintin haircut."

The kid said, "You lay a hand on me, my dad'll sue you. Take everything you own."

Ah, one of those…

Blake stepped over the trail of balled up pages from the magazine and gripped the boy's greasy mop and pulled him out of the room, through the hallway, and to the lobby. The kid shrieked as they passed the burning trash can:

"This isn't your world. Not anymore, bruh. This isn't your world."

Emilia opened the front door. Blake picked up the kid and aimed him for the street. "Go back to the art school," he said. "Make sure the other rich pricks know the new sheriff at Let's Chill ain't half as nice as Connell Riggins." Then he booted him hard enough to send him tumbling over the sidewalk. As the kid stood, he wiped dirt from his face and pointed at him.

"You'll hear from my dad. He's a lawyer."

"Thanks for the reminder." Blake let the door close. Emilia stood by the receptionist window. She'd crossed her hands in front of her belly, her thumbs picking at her cream-colored bikini bottom.

A duck boat rolled into the parking lot across the street. The army green paint it had once been covered with had chipped and peeled, exposing a dull, metallic shade. The roof had been removed. Two women in thongs and cutoff shirts exposing the lower halves of their volleyball-sized breasts danced in the passenger area. The amphibious vehicle parked near the concrete arch, covering three spaces. Mozo climbed out of the driver's seat and helped the women off the side. Blake searched for a clock in the lobby of the massage parlor. He asked Emilia if she had a watch. She slipped into the receptionist's office and dug through a violet backpack covered in 'tolerance' and 'diversity' stickers. She produced a smartphone twice the size of her hand. "About eight-thirty," she said.

"Mozo shows up same time, every night?"

She shrugged. "I guess so. He's usually at the bar by now."

"You familiar with him?"

"Of course," she said. "He rescued me."

Blake wanted to know what that meant. The youth, in 2017,

however, could get offended by *anything*.

Emilia sucked in her lips, like a child ashamed of saying something she felt she shouldn't have. She stuffed her phone into her backpack and excused herself. Down the hallway, two girls went to work on the burning trashcan with a fire extinguisher. They read the instructions and sprayed each other, giggling at the accident, before figuring out how to aim the nozzle at the wastebasket and spew chemicals into it. Blake climbed the fire escape to the roof and found Mina there, sitting on a folding lawn chair, a margarita glass in her hand.

"Didn't mean to disturb you."

"No worries," she said. "Connell and I used to chill up here and listen to the drummers and make out when Lalo ate his dinner."

Moving to the edge of the roof, Blake said, "Unusual place, this is."

"You'll get used to it."

"I don't know." He picked at a half-scab, half-pimple on his knee, wondered at what point in life acne stopped showing up on random body parts. "You sure there's nothing Connell said to you before he died? Nothing you might have found outrageous, disturbing?"

"I told you," she said, "he refused to see me those last few days."

"But you don't buy the suicide story."

"I'd never met a man who enjoyed life like Connell did. His optimism put even Mozo's zippity-doo-dah bullshit to shame."

"Mozo's attitude is pretty refreshing," said Blake. "Considering he survived a revolution. I mean, an actual revolution. Not some spoiled college kids refusing to take their midterms."

She nodded. "Connell did time in Iraq. He fought in the second battle in Fallujah. He said he'd had no idea how much blood a single human being could produce when hit in the right place with a bullet. Or maybe the wrong place, right? I guess when you've witnessed that kind of shit, you can either let it destroy you, or you can whistle and skip through whatever's left of your life. Maybe these men, Connell and Mozo, maybe they understand gratitude better than the rest of us."

"Can I tell you something?" said Blake. "You have to swear this will stay between us."

She sipped her sunset-colored drink. "Do you know me well enough?"

"I don't have a choice." He revealed the instructions he'd been given—to put deadly holes in Mozo's skull and act normal when the ensuing shitstorm erupted. "These people, they can do whatever they want. I refuse to cooperate, they'll help me commit suicide the same way they did Connell. Why shouldn't I believe they have a patsy in the wings?"

Mina stirred her drink with her pinky. She didn't look at him when she spoke. "It's true? They killed Connell?"

"I'm afraid so."

Shifting her right foot back and forth like a windshield wiper, creating a half-circle in the pebbles on the roof, she said, "Why don't you return the favor?"

"It's like we're in one of those *Twilight Zone* episodes where people are being messed with and, in the end, it turns out those people were toys for unseen giants." He mentioned his grandfather's obsession with power. How the few possessing it controlled the rest of the population. "These people, they're exactly what my grandpa was talking about."

"Tell Mozo," she said.

"I'm sure if I say something to him, they're going to kill me. No doubt about it. Just like Connell. And they'll get away with it."

"Then leave."

"No, no." He shook his head. "They got me by the balls—no offense. They got the one thing I had that allowed me to move about freely, do whatever I wanted."

She worked on her drink. The evening breeze picked up, as did the drumming from the beach. The ungodly sound of the sheep, bleating for mercy, cut through the air. They listened as the drumming reached its frenetic apex and the sheep's cutting cries ceased. "There it is," she said. "Lalo's satisfied."

Would she feel nostalgic? Give him a smooch, complete his substitution of Connell Riggins? He smiled. She shook her head 'no' with the kindest rhythm.

"I was thinking," said Blake. "What if there were some way to make it *look* like I'd done my job?"

"Shoot him in his leg?" She finished her drink.

"I don't know that I'm a good enough shot."

"Easy enough." She stood and folded her chair.

He waited for her to explain.

"Everything else on this island is an illusion." She winked as she passed him, leaving him in a Fendi cocoon.

Nine

The Renault had trouble turning over the next morning. Blake put the car in neutral and, standing outside the driver's seat, pushed it to the edge of the parking lot and onto the street. As soon as it gained momentum, he popped the clutch and the engine fired. He drove across the bridge to Sarasota, the rifle next to him on the passenger seat. He still had cash in his pocket. The sooner he took care of the task, the sooner he could demand his money from Don Stinson. Not that he expected him to comply. The rich didn't forfeit wealth without a struggle. They'd capitulated to unions in the early part of the twentieth century. Working folks thought they'd won the right to half an ounce of respect, only to watch sons of the rich bastards defeated the first time around return in the seventies and eighties to squash the unions once and for all. The battle between the doomed and the spoiled never ended. Blake knew neither communism nor capitalism would save the working class. The concentration of power had always been the same and would remain that way until a blessed asteroid slammed into the planet and put the species out of its misery. But he'd give it a go. See how Don Stinson squealed once he put bullets in his goons and his boy Ethan.

He found a shooting range and ammunition store in a strip mall between a Chuck E. Cheese and Hobby Lobby. A broad, autumn brown sign announced, Stacy's House of Bang! Blake mistook it, initially, for a brothel. Illustrated bullets flying from the barrel of an inflatable six-shooter hanging over the door clarified things. A neon-sign in the window indicated the joint's operating hours. He pulled into a space backward should he need to start the car manually when he left. He carried the case with the rifle under his arm. As he entered the store, he spotted security cameras mounted in all four corners of the showroom. He ducked his head, regretted not having a baseball cap to cover his eyes. Two people worked behind a long, glass display case filled with cartridges. He found himself wanting to talk to the manager, suggest if more human beings were hired, the security cameras wouldn't be necessary and the stripping away of privacy through surveillance could cease. But society, in general, had grown accustomed to it. Nobody cared anymore. If he'd brought up the subject with random strangers, they'd parrot the same, defeatist nonsense: "If you have nothing to hide, what are you afraid of?" He understood why intelligent people went crazy and did awful things to themselves and, sometimes, others.

He scanned the ammunition in the display case until he spotted what looked to be appropriate rounds for the rifle. One of the two employees, a woman in a tangerine bikini, bounced over. A nametag dangling from the left strap on her top introduced her as Lara. She twirled her fingers in her curly blonde hair. "What can I do you for?"

Blake placed the black case on the counter and opened it. "I was wondering what might work best for this."

The woman grimaced. "You get this as a gift from your grandpa?"

Snapping his fingers and pointing at her, he said, "Bingo."

She leaned down, cracked the sliding-door behind the counter, rummaged through several stacks of ammunition, and brought out two different boxes. "You planning on long or short distance?"

"Long distance. Want to make sure I leave my options open. I'd also like to take this antique for a test drive on your range this morning."

"Fantastic." She put one of the boxes back, then opened the other. "These are .308s. You can hit something half a mile away, if necessary."

He picked up one of the slender, narrow-tipped bullets. "Looks pretty serious."

"You ever use a rifle?"

He had. He'd feigned ignorance when Don Stinson had asked him the same question. He'd said, "Nope. Only trigger I ever pulled was on Crystal, my trusty .38." To which Don Stinson offered the following gem:

"Bull-pucky, son. You were born in Indiana. We crawl from our mamas' wombs with a long-gun in our hands, yes sir, locked and loaded from the get-go."

Blake had, in fact, fired shotguns at his Uncle Mike's farm outside of Buck Creek. He'd splattered wooden targets carved and painted to look like wild turkeys. Found it rather easy. Easier than the .38, whose kick couldn't guarantee where the slug might land. He told the woman at the counter he'd need some assistance. She said, "Sure thing." She closed the case holding the rifle and nudged it toward him. She picked up the box of ammo and grabbed a roll of paper resting in an ornate, golden umbrella holder. He walked with her around a corner to a dim corridor leading to a door. She fitted him with earmuffs and put on a pair of her own. Then they entered the range and found a free lane. She set the box of bullets on the wooden shelf and flipped a switch, held it in place. A target carrier whirred to them from the far end. She unrolled the paper she'd retrieved from the umbrella holder. The targets were poorly drawn sketches of popular democrats, including Hillary Clinton looking toward the sky with a demented gleam, Elizabeth Warren wearing a Native American headdress, and Bernie Sanders holding a clump of blood-soaked money in a hand with pointed fingernails. "Which of these commies you hate the most?"

Blake said, "I only hate killers of innocence."

"Aw, that's sweet." She clipped a caricature of Maxine Waters to the target carrier and sent it back a hundred feet. She showed him how to slide in the cartridges and explained how to clear the chamber after each shot. She fired two rounds, tearing a single hole in the center of the senator's face. Then she handed him the rifle.

Blake leaned over and aimed at a hammer-and-sickle-shaped broach sketched onto the senator's chest. The bullet tore through where he'd intended. "Oh," he said as he pulled the bolt handle and shoved another cartridge into position, "I like this." He sent a second bullet into the senator's throat.

"You're a natural," said Lara. "Ever thought about shooting professionally?"

He grinned. "I am looking for a new career in a new town."

She left him to finish off the box. He placed bullets in the hearts and minds of the NRA's finest enemies. He had nothing against the politicians in real life. They did what all politicians did—made promises to the doomed and forgot all about them as soon as they got into office. He'd never seen much difference between republicans and democrats. He'd have been just as content aiming at an artist's rendition of the Great Distractor, the orange celebrity in the White House who, along with the news channels owned by international corporations, compelled enough divisive contempt across the land to fuel a second civil war. Only a matter of time.

When he returned to the front showroom to pay for the bullets, targets, and his use of the range, he asked, "Do you have any blank cartridges?"

Lara's dimpled chin sank toward her giraffe-like throat. "Why would you want those?"

"I'm only interested in warding off potential trespassers for now. You know, fire a shot if you hear someone trying to break in. Old fashioned, I know. I don't want anyone I love accidentally getting hurt."

The woman studied him for a moment, as though she considered the conversation part of a script. She said, "Sure." She sifted through a stack of Winchester boxes and pulled one from the bottom. "These are basically fireworks without the pretty lights."

Over the previous two years of his life, Blake Ness had learned the invisible hands turning the world day by day were stained with enough blood to flood the oceans. They operated in the dark and they never paid for their crimes. Any time someone nosy crept too close, his nose got lopped off with a machete, along with his head and limbs. He'd developed a belief regarding so-called conspiracy theories: If three or more people associated with a controversy died under mysterious circumstances, the theory passed into the realm of fact. This meant the murder of John F. Kennedy by multiple shooters in Deeley Plaza could be called by its proper name: a coup d'état. No reason for an investigation. He had now met enough people working behind the scenes to know the worst suspicions, the ones earning scorn and labels of "paranoid" and "crazy" by the lazy, gutless masses, were usually true. In America, after time, those who perpetrated heinous acts didn't even bother hiding it. Activities of the CIA in the 1950s, once considered too outrageous to believe, were matters of public record by the beginning of the new century. Less than a hundred years and the puppet masters made it clear they didn't give a damn who knew about the filth they'd foisted upon the population, the stain they'd smattered across the nation's reputation with the rest of the world. Comfort in this knowledge allowed him the faith he needed to put on black clothes—a pair of denim jeans and a Motörhead tour shirt from 1991—and climb the fire escape with the rifle cradled close to his body. He rested on pebbles covering the roof behind the short ledge hanging over the sidewalk, wincing from sharp edges digging into his knees and elbows. He'd told Mina to avoid the roof that night, told her his plan to fire blanks at Mozo. "He'll survive an assassination attempt," he said. "That'll cement his reputation as a local god. People too young to understand what it meant to fight against the communists in Cuba will appreciate an old man somehow walking away from a bullet aimed at his skull."

Mina tried to talk him out of it. "What if these rich crudos lied to you? What if they're going to pin it on you, regardless?"

"What if?" he said. "It's not live ammo."

She didn't like it, but she agreed to stay away.

The air pulsated from the drumming. Blake's fingers sweat on the gun. He coached himself: "You've done much worse. This isn't even the real thing." Just an illusion, like Mina had suggested. Wallace pulled into the parking lot and offloaded the sheep on his truck. Not long after, the sloppy engine of the amphibious vehicle disrupted the rhythm from the beach. Blake raised himself, the pebbles now torturing his knees. He positioned the barrel of the rifle on the ledge and peered through the scope. He found Mozo, driving the duck boat, the top of his head covered by a Panama hat. The lucky bastard had four girls in thongs riding in the back of the vehicle. He parked across a striped area with the words *Absolutely No Parking* written in the center. The girls hopped out the side door and Mozo stepped from the cab. Blake centered the crosshair between Mozo's eyes. In his imagination, leading to that moment, he'd pictured himself taking a deep breath and counting down. Once he had the man's nose in the scope, however, he didn't blink before squeezing the trigger. The rifle cracked like hollow thunder, forced him to drop the gun and grab his ear. He rolled over the rough surface of the roof, cussing, until the ringing died down enough for him to hear screams from the beach. He peered over the ledge, still nursing his offended ear. The duckboat had been splashed with blood. A crowd stood in a semi-circle around the body of Mozo. Half the mayor's face had disappeared.

Ten

Blake returned the rifle to its case. He set it in the bottom drawer of the dresser, as Don Stinson had instructed. He'd also been told not to be there when the cops arrived. He knocked on Mina's door. She answered in a long T-shirt with pink stripes on the shoulders, like a football jersey, and the number sixty-nine on the front and back. She said, "Am I safe, being alone with you?"

"I loaded the rifle with blanks, for Christ's sake. The girl at the range sold me the wrong bullets. Maybe on purpose. Maybe she's incompetent. I don't know."

Stepping aside and letting him enter, she said, "Mozo paid the bills around here. We're totally screwed."

"Maybe that was the point." He sat on the queen-sized bed in the center of the room. A thick carob quilt covering the mattress smelled like her perfume. He had no idea why someone would need a quilt in Florida in the middle of summer. He found the remote control for a small, flat-screen television propped against the vanity mirror on a dresser whose legs were held together with electrical tape. Emergency vehicles and panic filled an open window to his left. He turned up the volume on the TV. "You get the local news channel, the one with Linda Lee?"

She took the control from him. "WLVE," she said as she punched the appropriate numbers. Linda Lee, her smooth, black hair tied in a ponytail, sat at her canary desk narrating a story about several men accused of kidnapping sandhill cranes and selling them to underground restaurants. Mina said, "Disgusting." The camera shook and Linda Lee tapped her ear.

"I'm sorry." She refocused on the teleprompter in front of her. "We're getting word now that a shooting has taken place on peaceful Raro Key. Let's join Jenny Eltern, who's just arrived on the scene."

The picture cut to a shot of the concrete arch leading to Lonesome Cowboy Bill's. The image panned right and a young woman in a seafoam-colored tank top fixed her auburn hair so it hung like stage curtains at the edges of her eyes. She spoke into a handheld microphone: "Linda, I'm at the Stargate, as locals call the entrance to the beach at Raro Key. Terror has occurred here tonight on an island where, normally, locals say, nothing much happens. Mozo Guerrero, the man who made Raro Key what it is today, was shot in the head by a sniper from the top of one of the businesses across the street." The camera swung one-hundred and eighty degrees. On its way around, a blur of sirens trailed from where Mozo had taken the bullet to the massage parlor and Trascendente. County sheriff vehicles lined the street. A flurry of uniformed officers hustled in and out of the building.

"Dammit." Blake rested his head in his hand. "I should have cut my losses, to quote Bible Boy, and headed south. Maybe I could have swum to Cuba and gotten a job translating late night jokes for whoever the hell is in charge down there."

"¿Hablas español?" said Mina.

"Nope."

She wandered to the window. "Oh my God. They're everywhere." Strobing red lights bounced off her eyes in chaotic rhythms. A knock fell on the door. Mina said, "Just chill."

Two deputy sheriffs stood in the hall. They removed their campaign hats. Both had shaved heads and fresh acne.

"Sorry to disturb you, ma'am," said the taller of the two. "In case you didn't notice, something serious has gone down."

His partner said, "The mayor's been killed."

"We saw that." She pointed to the television.

"We're going door to door, just checking things out." The taller deputy slithered into the room. His trained, paranoid gaze crawled over the furniture and clothes on the floor like a lion surmising a carcass.

The other deputy pointed a thumb at Blake. "You live here as well, sir?"

He should have been cooler. He told himself to remember his faith in the corrupt powers of the world. "I do."

Mina cleared her throat and glared at him.

"I live down the hall. Two-eleven."

The deputies looked at each other, then at Blake. The taller deputy said, "We've already checked out your place, sir." He held eye contact with Blake and nodded. Then he said to his partner, "Everything's good." He ambled toward the door, clipping his fingers to his partner's shirtsleeve and dragging him away. "There's a killer, somewhere on these premises." He waved his finger back and forth between Blake and Mina. "I'm going to have to ask you all to head on over to the beach and wait for us to signal it's cool for you all to return."

"Well," said Mina, "that's that." Her head swiveled between the hallway the deputies once occupied and the man on her bed. She sifted through a pile of clothes on her floor, found a pair of cut-off shorts and a Hello Kitty T-shirt. She excused herself and ducked into her bathroom. She did not close the door.

Blake stood and walked to the window. A sea of throbbing red lights stretched from the sidewalk to the concrete arch at the end of the parking lot. Unmarked vans lined the front of the building. Officers with surgical gloves entered and exited Let's Chill.

Mina returned from the bathroom and tossed her sixty-nine jersey onto her bed. She slipped her feet into a pair of crumbling flip-flops and said, "Let's mingle with the masses."

They navigated the maze of emergency vehicles. Blake steered them toward the duck boat. Two women in lab coats worked inside a square of yellow crime scene tape, measuring the distance between Mozo's body and the finger-painting swoosh of blood on the duck boat's driver's side door. Regular, uniformed police officers from Sarasota wrangled a crowd of yuppies. Most of the men and women in khaki shorts, Hawaiian shirts, and summer dresses nursed drinks from the bar, trying to peer over each other's shoulders. Blake wanted to blurt out, "It's all bullshit!" He turned to say so, just to Mina. She'd clasped her hand across her mouth, her eyes glued to the horrific sight of the old man on the ground, a chiseled bone and cartilage crater in the center of his face. He nudged her under her elbow and directed her to the concrete arch. They passed the WLVE crew, their lights and camera equipment placed without care for the heavy foot traffic filing in and out of the bar. Jenny Eltern puckered her lips into a compact mirror.

The older patrons of Lonesome Cowboy Bill's had clumped together near the television. Linda Lee sat at her canary desk looking even more dour and phony serious than usual. She said, "We're getting word police have a suspect in custody. White male, age undetermined. Obviously, armed and dangerous."

The rainbow-colored parrot, balancing itself on top of the television, said, *White male. White male. Dangerous white male.*

Blake scanned beyond the crowd. Hippies from the drum circle huddled near a far corner. The majority had been marked with scorpion tattoos by their bellies. Same as the kids at the castle. "Excuse me," he said to Mina. He pushed through the gazing zombies, wrinkled his nose at the stench of alcohol and rotten breath, and made his way to the hippies. Those who watched his approach tilted their heads. "Hey there." He tried to smile, something he hadn't done often in his life. "I hope Lalo got her, its, ah, what is Lalo, anyway? Male? Female?"

A young woman with three hoops in each of her nostrils rocked her head backward and slammed her fists into her hips. "What's *that* matter?" She'd tied the ends of her purplish dreadlocks with cloth adorned with images of Tinker Bell. "Lalo gets to determine its own gender, not you."

"Sure thing," said Blake. "Did Lalo get *its* meal?"

Joining the young woman with the Tinker Bell dreads, a young man who'd gone bald in the center of his skull and grown out the remaining strands on the sides and back said, "*Their.* Use the pronoun *their.* In that situation, it's their, bruh."

"Okay. Did Lalo get *their* meal?"

"No, he didn't," said the woman with the Tinker Bell dreads. "The excitement scared him away." She stepped aside, allowed Blake a view of the sheep, still staked to the ground on the beach.

"It's uncool," said her buddy. "Lalo isn't appeased, who knows what'll happen tonight?"

"Beach won't be safe," said a young woman with the word Brooklyn branded across her chest. A tattoo of a unicorn battled her scorpion from the other side of her belly button.

Blake said, "You from New York?"

"It's their name, *fascist*." The thin lips on the woman with the Tinker Bell dreads froze in a sneer. Her buddy, or boyfriend (theirfriend?) stroked her dreads the way a pet owner might calm a nervous cat.

Brooklyn massaged the woman's shoulders. When she spoke to Blake, she maintained a rational tone. "Last time Lalo wasn't appeased," she said, "so I've heard, at least, three people crashing on the beach were attacked. Lalo gets shitty, he doesn't get his food."

Pointing at the scorpion on Brooklyn's stomach, Blake said, "Interesting tattoo. You mind telling me where you got it?"

The woman's face collapsed. She shook her head, as though he'd suggested she snack on broken glass. She walked away with her head angled to the ground, rolling left and right, like a boulder between two peaks.

Tinker Bell's buddy said, "Bad move, bruh. You might have hit it off with her, you didn't crowd her space like that."

"I'm curious about the tattoo. No ill intentions, trust me."

"It unites us," said the young man. "And we don't trigger ourselves by talking about it."

The crowd near the television hushed per command of a woman in a long, white skirt and blouse. "Linda says they've got the bastard!"

Drunks filed out of Lonesome Cowboy Bill's. Mina waved to Blake to join her. He wished the hippies well. His exit appeared to make them neither happy nor sad. In the parking lot, the throng of middle-aged gawkers pushed and shoved to the edge of the street. Uniformed officers prevented them from going any further. Three unmarked vans had parked in the middle of the road. A man in a lab coat, wearing latex gloves, emerged from the massage parlor with a bolt-action rifle hoisted above his head. Even from a distance, Blake could see the differences between it and the weapon he'd used earlier. A woman in a lab coat carried a cardboard box to the man displaying the gun. They set the rifle into the box and loaded it into the van parked farthest from the building. Half a dozen law enforcement officials loitered in front of the massage parlor. They stepped aside as two men in navy blazers and blood-red ties led a man dressed in khaki pants and a camouflaged hunting jacket to another van. The man's hands were cuffed in front of him. A pillowcase pulled over his face hid his identity. The news crew from WLVE budged through the crowd, the cameraman holding the camera away from his body. Women around Blake muttered, agreeing the man whose face they could not see looked exactly like an assassin:

"Oh, he's *creepy*. He did it, for sure."

"He's got to be one of those right wing Christian lunatics you hear about on TV."

"They better not use mental health as an excuse this time."

Blake considered asking them how they'd gleaned so much information. Mina whispered, "Who do they think they're kidding?"

He said, "These sheep?"

She punched him in the shoulder. "The cops. They think people are going to fall for this?"

"They have every reason to believe they can do whatever they want."

The van carrying the patsy pulled a U-turn, forcing yuppies who'd gotten too close to the action to back up on the sidewalk. It sped toward the drawbridge connecting the island to Sarasota. The other vans, along with an escort of four Sarasota squad cars, chased after it. A host of crime scene investigators remained at the massage parlor and on the top of the building. Blake wanted to sneak in, see if they'd ransacked his room. Mina took his arm and suggested they return with the civilians to Lonesome Cowboy Bill's. As they weaved through the crowd, Blake saw women from the massage parlor near the entrance to the bar. He asked Chelo how they were doing.

"This pendejo has taken our livelihood," she said. "Don't you gabachos think before you do this crazy shit?"

"What makes you think it was one of us?" He felt stupid, playing innocent.

She scoffed.

He returned to Mina and stood among a herd of people focused on the TV. Linda Lee, looking constipated, said, "I repeat, we have the name of the suspect in the shooting on Raro Key." A picture took her place on the screen, a man in his early fifties. Her voice continued, "Police have just released this information. The alleged terrorist is right-wing conspiracy theorist and propagandist Gordon Lane."

Blake studied the sand-covered, wooden floorboards. *Gordon Lane*. He'd heard the name before, in his previous life. He closed his eyes, desperate to ignite middle-aged brain cells, open the vault on his increasingly limited short-term memory. Not heard, *seen*. He'd *seen* the name on billboards and ads on the backs of bus stop benches in Indianapolis. Gordon Lane had been, according to those advertisements, a best-selling self-help author. Gordon Lane had never, as far as he knew, been referred to as "right-wing." Once again, however, the upper-class women in the crowd set him straight:

"I heard about him on CNN."

"Rachel Maddow did a whole spiel. Said his book was veiled racism and misogyny."

"If Rachel says he's a racist, he's a racist."

The rainbow-colored parrot squawked, *Racist! Racist! He's a racist!*

Blake wondered whether it might not be too late to tie one of the upper-class twits to the stake out on the beach. Lalo would understand, wouldn't he? A sheep is a sheep is a sheep. He said to Mina, "Ever heard of this guy?"

"Never read *Mein Kampf*," she said. "Why would I read his shit?"

On the television, an expert from South Florida University had been brought in via Skype to discuss the monster responsible for killing Mozo. According to overlays underneath his fractured image, Eric Hinterpeck specialized in Cultural Studies. He wore square glasses, frames the size of playing cards, washed out from his computer screen's glow. He spoke in the posh, arrogant tones Blake's father and his fellow professors from Butler University had at Thanksgivings, when his father invited colleagues over for what they called Feast of the Grateful Thieves. They'd go around the table admonishing themselves for the color of their skin. Blake made the mistake, one year, of asking if any of them had ancestors on the Mayflower. His father sent him to his room and beat him after his colleagues had gone home. He whipped him with his belt in four stages. He began with one and said that accounted for little Blake's "overwhelming historical ignorance." He then gave him four swift whacks, whereupon the abuse began to hurt. "The four stands for our murderous *fore*fathers." And then he whipped him nine slow, painful, methodical times. "Nine is divisible by three, three being a significant number in the bloodthirsty Christian faith." He ended with a pair of slicing attacks and explained the group of one, four, nine, and two heralded the genocidal landing of Christopher Columbus. His father insisted he would never amount to anything if he didn't atone for the sins of the past.

Dr. Hinterpeck said, "Gordon Lane's bestseller, *Breaking Glass*, was embraced by the alt-right as soon as it hit the stands. It's one of these capitulating tomes by closet fascists. On the surface, the book appears to be critical of liberals *and* conservatives. This ignores the basic truth that liberals are immune to criticism. David Duke praised the book, suggesting it could bring the country together. Calls for unity from the right are always veiled affirmations of White Supremacy."

Linda Lee said, "How so?"

The professor grumbled a bit and adjusted his tie. "Are you defending a Nazi?"

Linda Lee blushed and apologized with flustered pleas appropriate for a criminal facing the guillotine.

"Was the mayor of Raro Key a minority?" The professor's severe, rectangular eyebrows peeked over the rims of his glasses.

"Yes," said Linda Lee.

"We have a white suspect," said the professor. "Our victim is a person of color. It's an open-and-shut case. If I had things my way, the Nazi would be receiving lethal chemicals through an IV at this very moment."

Linda Lee mumbled something about due process.

"Due process is for *civilized* human beings." Eric Hinterpeck adjusted his glasses. "Fascists are animals. They should be treated as such."

The rainbow-colored parrot said, *Fascists! Fascists! Nazi fascists!*

Murmurs floated through the crowd, mostly the upper-class, middle-aged women agreeing Gordon Lane should be executed that night. Blake and Mina had gone back to sit with the women from the massage parlor. None of them seemed interested in discussing anything other than how they would pay their bills, should Mozo not have left a will or anything else designed to keep the island's businesses open. He asked Mina what she would do.

"Guess I'll go live with my sister in Miami." She didn't appear upset by the prospect. "I kind of lost interest in running the store once Connell died. Might be the perfect thing for my depression."

A sheriff's deputy entered the bar and demanded attention. He announced all clear for the women to return to the massage parlor. Blake inquired whether he and Mina could enter the building. "We've got everything we need," he said to Blake. He might have winked, or maybe his eye twitched involuntarily.

Blake walked Mina to her apartment, asked if she needed company. She said, "Wouldn't be a good idea, would it?"

He raised his hands and retreated to his room. Once he'd closed his door, he stared at the dresser. He knelt in front of it and pulled out the lowest drawer. The black case holding the rifle and the box of ammunition he'd been told contained blanks were missing. He opened his shoebox, which had been put in their place, and confirmed his money had been returned.

Eleven

Blake lay on his bed, listened to the rafters creak and moan. Crystal rested on his chest, ready to spit death, should the law or Don Stinson's goons bust in and decide to arrest or silence him. He sought the ghost's counsel and received a curt response:

"You are no better than them."

The ghost had the decency to provide power to the transistor radio. The Big Band station, however, had become consumed with chatter over the assassination. Had the nation taken notice? Providing he survived the night, he would have to duck into an establishment with a cable or satellite hookup and get a sense of how serious the shooting appeared to eyes beyond Sarasota.

On the radio, a woman with a frail, shaky voice said, "It's not surprising we now have Nazis killing colored people in our streets. Not in the environment created by you-know-who." She must have been referring to the president, a bloviating greedhead who'd convinced blue collar America he gave a shit about them. The president looked and sounded like every frat boy Blake Ness had ever put in his place—the Skeeters and the Zacks and the Chets and the Chads of the world. The president had bullied his way into the office by refusing to follow any rules of decorum. He snorted porn-star pussy-scented cocaine off Wall Street's balls and plowed the doomed with Darwinian glee. Wouldn't have bothered Blake, were it not for the fact that underneath all the huffing and puffing, beyond the moronic tweets the president sent out any time he wanted to rile the grievance junkies on the left, yes, underneath all his unattractive traits, the man consisted of nothing but bullshit. That didn't stop the roundtable of wealthy leftists on the radio from deeming the current president and his supporters worse than the occupying force in Germany eighty years earlier, responsible for the systematic murder of several million Jews, Masons, and other so-called undesirables. The current president possessed the attributes of a buffoon, for sure, but he had yet to match the murderous ferocity of Stalin or Mao Zedong. To lump him in with history's most efficient killers could only be described as uninformed hyperbole.

A man whose voice sounded as though it had been unsteady since the Eisenhower administration said, "This fellow, this Gordon Lane, he was a best-selling author. That means tons of people bought into his tripe." Someone at the table asked if anyone had read Gordon Lane's book. Scoffs all around. Not one person had the sense to suggest they should at least take a look at it before drawing conclusions. The same man said, "I lived through World War II. I know what horrors lurk in this ideology." Then, without a hint of awareness, he said, "We need to find the people who've tasted this man's poison and eliminate them. They're parasites. A threat to national security."

Blake said, "Can you change the channel?"

The beams overhead groaned twice.

He walked over to the radio to turn it off. The radio refused to die. He attempted to tune it to a different station. The dial wouldn't move. "You're not teaching me anything," he said to the ghost.

"I'm not trying to teach you, buddy. I'm trying to annoy you."

Blake offered light applause. "Mission accomplished." He leaned over the dresser and peeked through the blinds. The panther from the first night had stopped in the middle of the street and stared, it seemed, right back at him. Then the panther turned its head and emitted a gentle growl as a larger, heavier panther joined it. They lingered in the road, glanced up, and walked together into the darkness beyond the beach. "You win." Blake returned to the bed. "I'll listen to the decaying hypocrites."

The radio went silent. Blake folded his hands across Crystal and tried to find peace in the odd sounds drifting in from the outside—the ocean, lapping at the shore in its lazy, gulf manner, a minor symphony of night animals, chirping, buzzing, communicating things to each other, possibly the end of the world.

Sleep arrived just before the sun broke across the land and bled scarlet shapes on the floor. The radio crackled to life around the same time and the decrepit DJs bemoaning Nazis behind every tree had retired to their condos. The station resumed the medicinal comfort of Frank Sinatra, Dean Martin, Glenn Miller, Tommy Dorsey, the Ray Conniff Orchestra, for Christ's sake. Blake had slipped into a dream, a memory, if he were to be honest, of Lita Fisher, the only woman he'd ever asked to marry him. They'd met in high school, though she refused to commit, played pinball between him and the school's valedictorian, an automaton whose parents, having come from Louisiana, gave their four, Aryan sons pretentious French names. Lita, ultimately, had been interested in money. While she enjoyed what Blake did for her physically, the financial prospects of the valedictorian kept her, momentarily, unsure, until the valedictorian, in an effort to appease Lita Fisher's faux hippie veneer, volunteered to move to Wyoming and work on the Wind River reservation. Lita dropped him and pledged herself to Blake, who had taken a job driving gumball machines across the country. She would read books by Margaret Atwood and Sylvia Plath and insist they applied to her own life. She subjected Blake to copious dime store psychoanalyses based on *Cosmo* articles she'd taken seriously. He couldn't bar his young libido from chasing her, from wanting to spend his life with her, thinking he could put up with her monthly inquisitions as long as she provided thrills of equal intensity in bed. The dream he'd had, a common one, shuffled the events of the day she'd informed him she intended to marry another man. A wealthier man. In the dream, they sat in a Waffle House on 54th Street, near the north side of Indianapolis. She slurped on a tall sundae with an exaggerated tongue. When he uttered a noise of disapproval, she removed his eyeballs, whose pupils morphed into tiny mouths, and forced them to lick bleeding wounds on her skin. Blake did not believe in Freudism and felt dreams had no major significance. He understood his mind had failed to reconcile Lita Fisher's rejection and occasionally returned to the subject while he slept to find a way to justify her actions and file the event, permanently, in his mind's cellar, where all recollections no longer relevant gathered dust. This dream haunted him as he woke to Frank Sinatra suggesting he and someone else would meet again, though he had no idea where or when.

The previous day's events occupied his thoughts as he dressed and prepared to head down to Deep Fried Heaven. If Don Stinson had taken care of everything, as it appeared he had, nothing held Blake on Raro Key. He placed his .38 in the shoebox with his money, loaded his clothes into his gym bag, and left his room. Before descending the fire escape, he knocked on Mina's door. She didn't answer. He tapped several more times before the woman's groggy, irritated voice disrupted the still air:

"*What?*"

"Just wanted to say goodbye."

She stumbled across her floor and opened her door. Her hair twisted in a thousand directions. She'd stuffed herself into a pair of tiger-striped yoga pants that would not have looked out of place at a Ratt concert in 1984. "What did you say?"

"I'm taking off. South. Maybe Cuba. Maybe El Salvador."

She scratched at her eyebrow. "Are you stupid? You can't just go to South America."

"I don't see why not."

"They've decided this Nazi, what's his name? Barry Gordon?"

"Gordon Lane."

"They've decided he shot Mozo. Seems to me you have nothing to worry about."

"I got worse things to dodge."

Sliding her arm up the doorframe and propping herself on her elbow, she said, "So that's it? I mean, who knows what's going to happen to us, I mean, the diner, the massage parlor. All of us could be homeless tomorrow. You don't care?"

"Thought you were going to Miami?"

"That doesn't help the others."

"Not my concern."

She backed into her room and slammed the door.

He descended the fire escape, cursing the pain it brought his knees, and made his way to the diner. He took a seat at the counter, resting the shoebox on the stool next to him and the gym bag at his feet. Koko had been reading a newspaper, letting Polly May lounge on the pass-through's metal shelf. She folded the paper and said good morning. As she scooped up her spider and placed it on her shoulder, she said, "What's with all the extra stuff?"

"Taking off," said Blake.

"You ain't worried about the employment situation, are you hon?" She produced her cigarettes, knocked one out of the pack, and lit it. "Mozo's got someone to take care of us. I'm sure of it. The man slept with more women than Wilt Chamberlain. He ain't got kin running around somewhere on this planet, surprised wouldn't describe my reaction."

"Nah." Blake ordered his usual, waited for Koko to send the request back to the kitchen. "The massage parlor stays open, they can find someone else to eighty-six the perverts. Plenty of strapping young fellows on the beach. I'm sure they'd prefer living in an apartment for free."

"Those boys ain't got any gump to them." She used her cigarette to point toward the ocean. "Them and the girls, they were ruined a long time ago. Mozo let them crash on the beach because he felt sorry for them."

"How do you mean, ruined?"

"Tampered with," she said. "As in, when they were kids, somebody diddled them. Touchers, wealthy pricks. Sick sons of bitches who think molesting children gives them some sort of cosmic power. Real sick stuff, let me assure you."

"Sounds sick."

"Almost as sick as this crap they're telling us about Mozo's killing." She used her free hand to pick up the newspaper and rattle it. "Gordon Lane? How stupid do they think they've made us?"

"You don't buy it?"

"Hon, I read Gordon Lane's book two years ago. He ain't no right-winger and he sure as hell ain't a Nazi. His whole deal is getting people to shed all the baggage society drops on them so they can live better lives."

"Sounds harmless."

"In a world where the government wasn't trying to kill off us working folks, that might be true." She ashed in the sink. "Last thing our fearless leaders want is us thinking enough to spot all the phony tribalism dividing us, keeping us in a victim competition, looking for pity instead of being strong and self-reliant."

"That sounds conservative to me," said Blake.

"That's what they want you to think."

"That doesn't mean Gordon Lane couldn't have gone bonkers and decided to shoot somebody."

Koko smiled. She stroked Polly May's back with fingernails painted the colors of a candy cane. "Maybe you can answer me on this one, hon…How you going to tell me a man who's been in a coma for the last year could wake up, drive down here to sunny Florida, and snuff Mozo? A man, I suspect, Gordon Lane never heard of before and has zero reason to hold a grudge against, the kind of grudge powerful enough to bring a man to kill another?… How you going to tell me that's possible? How you going to say that without busting out laughing at your own stupid?"

The cook rang the bell and slid Blake's breakfast onto the metal shelf. Koko retrieved it and set it in front of him. She said, "Gordon Lane's book opened my eyes, got me to stop blaming other people for mistakes I'd made. When I heard he'd been beaten into a coma, I read every story that flashed across the Internet. And there weren't much, let me tell you. Newspapers said some gangbangers broke into his house and beat him and his wife—killed the wife, by the way. Now, I been suspicious of the whole thing, knowing how them who work behind the curtain don't like anybody with useful advice getting useful words out to the general public. I been thinking, the last year, the government put Gordon Lane into that coma. Hell, they might have paid off his wife. She might be living it up in the Bahamas or something. Now, I know for sure, the government wants to get rid of Gordon Lane. I been checking the Internet every day for news on him coming out of his coma and so far, nothing. But somehow, someway, that man was on Raro Key last night, with a gun, shooting at the mayor? You believe that, I got you a nice bridge in Brooklyn I'll sell you for a dime."

"Why the government?"

She finished her cigarette, ran water over it, and dropped it in the sink. "Government's just a generic word I use. Government ain't nothing with legs these days. It's money. Whoever's got money is in charge, and there's no convenient word for that."

"You said Gordon Lane would be coming down here from somewhere else?"

She nodded.

"Coming down from where?"

She put her hand on her hip, aimed her nose toward the ceiling and said, "Middle of nowhere. Also known as Indianapolis."

Blake wandered into Trascendente for one last chat with Ginger. Her thin hands shook as she negotiated a broom across the hardwood floor. Not that there appeared to be a grain of dirt on it. She'd worn a long, navy skirt and a loose, button-down blouse. Her initial glance at him carried judgment. Blake suspected she knew he'd been the triggerman, suspected her dice had somehow told her. She tilted her head and the sun barreling through the front window lifted shadows from her face, softening her appearance. She continued sweeping, didn't look at him as she spoke. "You are either a fool or a magician."

"I'm taking off," he said.

"Don't blame you." Her voice trembled, cracked, as though she might cry. She set the broom in the corner near the empty shelves and straightened her shoulders as she walked behind the counter. Resting her hands on a paperback book turned upside down, she said, "Things could get ugly around here. Mozo's reputation was always enough to maintain order." She covered her mouth to stifle a cough. "Well, beyond the ruffians in the massage parlor you were hired to deal with. But now? Who knows? They say Mozo has a next of kin, but nobody knows who the heck it is."

"What'll you do?" said Blake.

"Guess I'll head up to Tampa, call it a life. See if my son will help pay for me to sit in one of those retirement homes. I'll watch

Jerry Springer until my heart gives and they bury me with the flowers." This made her smile, for whatever reason.

"I can't imagine you being happy in a retirement home."

"Gosh, who the heck would be? Don't really have a choice."

Thin strings between Blake's heart and his conscience vibrated, compelled a sadness for this woman he barely knew. To give her purpose, he asked if she might tell his fortune one last time.

"Don't much see the point," she said as she retrieved the velvet sack with the dice. "I suppose a quickie wouldn't hurt." She winked at him and dumped the dice onto the counter.

He picked them up and rolled them. One tumbled just outside the circle. The other two landed with a single dot facing up.

"You like to be difficult, don't you?" She retrieved the runaway die and put it back in the bag. "You've just invited more trouble." She placed a finger on each of the remaining dice. "Always with the snake eyes, Mr. Ness. Understand, the number two is the number of deception."

"Doesn't surprise me."

"Raro Key is no different than the rest of the world," she said. "Your eyes will deceive you more times than not. Your heart and mind behave the same. Imagine one man trying to make sense of so many in-house liars. I do not envy you, Mr. Ness."

Blake cussed as he jumped into the car and kick-started the engine. He'd tossed the gym bag into the back and shoved the shoebox underneath the passenger seat. Getting across the bridge took time as traffic had stacked. TV news vans and nosy tourists. Sheriff's deputies stood on the sidewalks lining the edges of the bridge. As he passed a stocky deputy wearing mirrored shades, the man tipped his campaign hat, specifically, to him. Combined with the deputy's grin, Blake imagined him saying something like, "That's right, pard'ner, you just roll as far away from here as possible."

Once traffic moved, Blake stepped on the gas and almost failed to notice the Chuck E. Cheese and Hobby Lobby surrounding the ammunition store that had sold him live rounds. He smashed his foot into the brake pedal when the radio underneath the busted climate control crackled and tuned itself to the Big Band station.

Drivers in the cars behind him honked. The volume of the music decreased and the ghost said, "Notice anything unusual?"

Blake pulled into the parking lot of the strip mall, right up to the building he'd been in twenty-four hours earlier. Everything about the establishment had changed—the blacked-out windows were now clear. Inside, men and women in somewhat casual office clothes sat at open desks, working on small computers. The inflated gun no longer dangled under the sign above the store which now read, Dolent Enterprises. He shut off the car and got out. As he opened the glass door and stepped into the refurbished business, the employees looked over in unison, like robots. He thought of *Invasion of the Body Snatchers*, the original and the one with Spock, both being, in his mind, competent movies. He thought of *Village of the Damned* and *Children of the Damned*. He thought of numerous episodes of *Twilight Zone* he'd seen in grade school. The workers at Dolent appeared to have been hatched in a laboratory, the men dressed in slacks and white, short-sleeved button-down shirts. They must have had coupons for the same barber who'd convinced them to slick their hair to their skulls like helmets. They wore thick, Morrissey glasses and carried a host of pens in their breast pockets. The colors of the women's one-piece dresses varied from beige to manila. Some had draped shawls over their shoulders and, in contrast to the men, they corrected their vision issues with horn-rimmed glasses fashionable only to the most self-loathing modern hipsters. A squat woman shaped like a potato sack wove around her desk and approached Blake the way he imagined Martians might someday greet human explorers in space. She said, "May I help you?" Her tone implied she had no interest in being anything but combative.

He said, "What happened to the gun range?"

The workers' necks stretched at the word gun. A woman near the back, seated next to a poster of a sprawling golf green, said, "Good golly, you'd think after what happened on Raro Key yesterday you NRA goons would take a day's rest."

Others agreed with her. Blake considered telling the woman to stick her head in an oven. He compared her and her colleagues to the parrot by the television set in Lonesome Cowboy Bill's. "Yesterday," he said, "this was a gun range."

A skeletal man adjusted a sky-blue clip-on tie dotted with sketches of Mickey Mouse. He stood and wedged himself between Blake and the potato-shaped woman. "Sir, this is a private business. I'm going to have to ask you, kindly, to leave."

Men like him always annoyed Blake. To call them men, in the first place, exhibited undue charity. These creatures inhabiting the *form* of men had never once fought to save their own lives. They'd never starved. They'd never struggled for one goddamn thing. They'd relied on stronger men to look after them, as though they were children, expecting, first, the police, and then the government to protect them from nastier challenges. When in doubt, they consulted lawyers and launched bureaucratic inquisitions to smite their enemies. Their spines, he suspected, were held together with paperclips. But, he decided, this imitation of a man standing before him had essentially been tasked with the same job Blake performed at the massage parlor. That he had the courage to utter his passive-aggressive command warranted a minute measure of respect. Blake said nothing as he turned and exited the building.

Rolling the Renault toward the street, he tried, but failed, to pop the clutch. He swung the steering wheel and annoyed his lower back as he forced the car to make a U-turn so he could give it another go. He wore out his legs and his arms attempting to fire the engine. Whatever ailed the French beast, healing it required someone with greater automotive knowledge. He surveyed the busy road and spotted a gas station with a garage a few blocks west. After pausing to recoup his strength, he switched on the blinkers and pushed it into traffic. As he endured a cacophony of honking horns and profanity, the dead radio came back to life. Vera Lynn sang "We'll Meet Again." He said, hoping the ghost would respond, "If you can make the radio work, why can't you get the car to run?"

"Sorry, buddy. That's not my jurisdiction."

His body ached as he passed an In-and-Out garage. No national chains. Those businesses came from or were involved with Big Money. And Big Money had nothing but blood all over it. Instead, he dug into his reservoir of endurance and wheeled the car to a

greasy garage with a busted, once-rotating sign on the corner—
Mitch's. The pumps out front had rounded edges, like they'd been
installed before the Vietnam War. No place to swipe a credit card.
No digital displays. No information transmitted to any centralized
authority. The radio in the car went silent as a rail-thin elderly man
emerged from the small lobby to the right of the two-bay garage.
Oil and goop spotted his Street blue coverall like paint on an artist's
drop cloth. White hair poked from under a ball cap with an oval
logo so faded it couldn't be discerned. He whistled at the Renault
as Blake brought it to a halt in front of the first bay door.

"Ain't seen one of these little toasters in, shoot, least a decade."
He walked around the car, his hand massaging his chin. "How
much you want for it?"

Blake leaned against the driver's side and caught his breath. "I
can't get it to start. Not even the fun way."

"Let's peek inside, shall we?" The old man tapped the hood
with his knuckles.

Blake released the lever under the driver's wheel. The top
popped and the old man whistled again.

"Never thought I'd miss these." He bent cables and ducked left
and right, surmising the engine the way Blake imagined a surgeon
evaluated a patient's guts before going to work with a scalpel.
"Nowadays, everything's covered, everything's computers." The old
man lifted himself to get a closer look. His legs teetered in the air.
"Oh, get yourself a peek at this." He pointed to what appeared to be
a small light-switch dangling on a line. He explained it determined
whether the engine fired without having to pop the clutch. He
flipped it to the 'on' position and invited him to put the key in the
ignition. The engine turned. Blake left it running while he thanked
the old man. "What do I owe you?" He sifted through a fold of
bills he'd stuffed in his pocket.

Holding up one hand in a 'stop' gesture, the old man said,
"Didn't take me but two seconds to figure it. No need to rob a man
who's made an enemy as clever as this." He nodded at the switch.
"That there's no factory installation. Somebody put that in on their
own. Trying to keep you from going anywhere. Or maybe just to
mess with your head." He tapped a knuckle against his temple.

Blake pulled into traffic and drifted in short, controlled bursts, toward the onramp for 75 South. The thin strands between his heart and conscience no longer vibrated. Someone had yanked them, maybe hoped they'd snap and Blake Ness would flee the country. Something in his DNA, however, prevented him from taking the safest path. At the last possible moment, he whipped onto the opposite ramp, the ramp heading *north*.

Twelve

The ghost kept things interesting by randomly tuning the radio without Blake's permission. As he approached the state line, the radio landed on a rare, left-leaning talk station. Two women volleyed opinions of Gordon Lane in breathy, cough syrup tones. They presumed Mozo a democrat. One of the women, her voice indistinguishable from the other, said, "He was a man of color and, from what I've heard, integrity. What else could he possibly be?"

Her partner said, "Why else would a Nazi murder him?"

They then discussed Gordon Lane's first book, *Breaking Glass*. They promised they had not read it, merely a description of it on Amazon. The first woman called it a "White Supremacist screed disguised as a Darwinian bullyfest."

Blake said, "You got to be kidding me."

The ghost said, "This is the new intelligentsia, buddy. No empirical knowledge? No problem."

As Blake drifted into Georgia, dense forests on the sides of the road opened to broad fields obscured by billboards advertising truck stop massage parlors. The near-comatose women on the radio cheered the efforts of social media and bookstores and, worst of all, Gordon Lane's publisher, to banish his work from legitimate scrutiny. The second host said, "Ragnar Books has announced they will not distribute Gordon Lane's latest diatribe, a vile waste of ink and paper called *Destination Manifesto*."

Her partner chimed in with an exaggerated sigh.

"Yeah," the second host continued, "that title tells you all you need to know."

"Let's be clear," said the first host. "Ragnar Books puts out nothing but Nazi propaganda. Every conservative blowhard I know of is with them. But it's nice to see even a Nazi knows when one of its own has gone too far."

"And let's be honest," said the other host. "What a joy it is to watch them eat each other."

"Indeed, indeed."

Blake tried to turn off the radio. Neither knob did anything. He said to the ghost, "Silence the damn thing or find someone on the air with half an IQ."

"Sure thing, buddy."

The dial moved to a pop country station. Some moussed up, tattooed poser blathered through a voice modulator about partying in a pickup truck. Blake imagined the ghost of Hank Williams coming back to life, tracking down every *GQ*-approved douchebag propped up by the corrupt music industry, putting a rusted Colt pistol to their temples, and pulling the trigger. At one point, the dickless turd on the radio rapped over a half-assed resonating guitar solo. Blake had argued with Chelsea Farmer about the difference between real country music and the shit Nashville peddled. He explained how pop country constituted nothing more than an attempt to recreate Mariah Carey songs with a fiddle and banjo. He offered to take her to a Dale Watson concert so she could witness the difference. She said she'd never heard of him. "Of course not," he said. "They don't want your generation knowing what the hell real goddamn country music is." Not that it should have mattered to him. He'd spent his youth listening to punk rock and heavy metal. As a blue-collar schlep in Indianapolis, he relied on Debussy and Miles Davis to calm his nerves after eighteen hours on the road. He simply knew, having driven gumball machines across the nation in the early 1990s, there existed radio stations that played Hank Snow, Lefty Frizzell, Patsy Cline, Dorothy Montana, and all the other people who'd built country music. The sound of an Ernest Tubb song took him to that time in his life, and it felt good. He'd been miserable, but he'd had hope, hope that someday he'd meet a woman as mesmerizing as Lita Fisher who didn't care about his lack of wealth. They'd get married, have kids. Eventually, his hard work and discipline would earn him a livable wage and he'd look at himself in the mirror and see an All-American middle-class success, a living Norman Rockwell painting. Chelsea had offered up the usual nonsense about pop country representing "progress" and any resistance to it, in turn, representing a "reactionary" gesture bordering, somehow, on racism, or one of the other isms or phobias college kids hurled at each other the way monkeys flung shit.

She'd said, "You're a traditionalist. Tradition is for dinosaurs."

Not long after that argument, he'd allowed a group of corrupt IMPD officers to rape her in the projection booth at a drive-in. Then he'd sold her to a rich man collecting damaged women for the entertainment of his wealthy friends. A despicable act, for sure. If he thought about it for too long, he overcame his aversion to remorse and beat himself up for it. Of his token concessions to her, his attempts to make up for this horrific act, he'd shot her Uncle Sewell in his face. That, he enjoyed reminding himself, made him feel no guilt whatsoever.

"All right," he said to the ghost. "I'll listen to the hens cluck on about this Nazi guy, Gordon Lane. Anything but this pop country shit."

"You got it, buddy."

The dial returned to the women bemoaning the notion that anyone in the world could possibly have an opinion different from theirs. He endured their myopia until the signal faded and the radio tuned itself to an Atlanta hip-hop station. Traffic clustered and he managed to ignore the lazy rhymes and complete lack of creativity marring contemporary rap music as he negotiated the psychotic, twisting freeways bisecting the city. The sun melted into the western horizon. He trudged on to Chattanooga and found a roadside motel that would take cash.

The Sweet Dixie Inn appeared to have been built just after the turn of the twentieth century. Tintypes of confederate soldiers hung crooked on the oak paneled walls of the cramped lobby. Life had beaten the man behind the caged window into a c-shape, forcing him to crane upward to address guests. Blake asked for a room and the man took his time responding. "You alone?" he said.

Blake nodded.

"You're not going to do anything freaky, are you? You look like one of these guys might decide to snort a pile of coke and shoot himself in the head."

"As awesome as that sounds," said Blake, "I don't have the courage to take my own life." Then he leaned closer, made sure he had the old man's attention. "Other people's lives? Well, that's another story."

This elicited a chuckle from the old man, followed by a thirty-second coughing gag. When he finished, he produced a soggy handkerchief from his back pocket. The tiny square of fabric might once have been white. Phlegm and other delights had painted it a curious shade between neon green and gray. He folded it up and returned it to his pocket. "You got a sense of humor like those old Bugs Bunny cartoons. No sympathy for civility."

"I take that as a compliment." Blake flashed his fold of money so the clerk understood he represented no fiscal threat. "How much for a single, one night?"

"You going to need a girl?" The old man wiped his nose with his thumb. "I can call you over a girl. Fat girl. Skinny girl. I got flavors, if'n you like flavors. Black girls. Asian girls. Even got a line on a Native American. You like girls, don't you?"

"I love women," said Blake. "Another time, I might have taken you up on that. Right now, I just need a good night's rest."

The clerk slid him a clipboard with a small stack of paper attached to it. The register had been hand-drawn, blue lines with names scribbled in such obvious haste, no investigator would ever discern who'd stayed there. Blake added to the visual gibberish, his signature no more than a series of dips and dives. The old man said, "Got an ID?"

"You don't need to see my identification." He counted out five twenties and set them on the counter. Pointing to his car, just outside the lobby, he said, "That's my Renault. You got my autograph. I'm giving you a deposit of a hundred bucks. We're square, far as I'm concerned."

"Whatever." The old man turned to a mounted board with keys hanging off hooks. He chewed on his bottom lip as he considered the nine available rooms. "Have number four. Not too many murders took place in there over the years."

"Now you're talking." Blake took the key and left the old man during a second coughing gag. He wondered how long he'd have to stay in Chattanooga to witness the clerk's natural passing. He drove the Renault around the rectangular, one-story building and parked between two Penske moving trucks.

The room had a queen-sized bed. His gym bag landed on the mattress with an alarming thud. He set his money and .38 on a nightstand with a rusted lamp on it. A humpbacked television sat on a dresser with three crooked drawers. He found a preseason football game on TV between the Chargers and Rams. He noticed both teams had relocated to Los Angeles. As he lay back on the bed and watched rookies beat the shit out of each other, he floated into hypnagogia. Chelsea Farmer, twenty-two years old, dressed in tight, black yoga pants and a pastel blouse clinging to her shoulders, appeared in front of the TV and crawled onto the bed with him. She rubbed his chest, asked him what he'd been up to. "I put your Uncle Sewell in the cemetery," he said. She smiled, her young, perfect teeth blinding him.

She said, "That's a good start."

His eyes closed and his mind dredged memories of the men he'd pimped Chelsea Farmer to—frat boys, business dorks, geezers. At the time, he'd given her feelings no consideration. She'd become a product. He wound her up with alcohol and watched her stagger across front walks and lawns and into apartment buildings where she exchanged sex for money. Sure, he retrieved her from the rich man shortly after he sold her to him and, yes, he'd ended Uncle Sewell's reign of vile, disgusting terror. Had that been enough? His voice replaced Chelsea Farmer's voice and he asked himself, "Do you enjoy killing?"

Lita Fisher now straddled him. Lita Fisher, at nineteen, when Blake asked her to marry him. "All that rage," she said, "all that anger. Why in the world would a woman with half a brain settle for you?"

"Love?"

She smirked. "Take that to the bank. See what they give you."

"You could have been honest," he said. "You could have told me who you really were. You wasted several years of my life, years I could have spent looking for a less materialist…"

"Don't give me that shit," she said. "I can't stand twerps like you who think a girl's supposed to swoon just because a guy has 'good intentions.'" She made quotes with her fingers. "Nobody has a right to insist someone else join them in a life of poverty and misery. I made a decision. Clearly, I made the right decision."

He couldn't argue. How could a beautiful, intelligent young woman like her possibly enjoy a front row seat for the sordid biography of Blake Ness? A violent, pulsating light signaled a headache and a voice, the ghost, perhaps, said, "Lita Fisher gave form to your bitterness, but even she's not responsible for your total lack of empathy."

Blake suggested the killing of the child molester, Uncle Sewell, had been an act of *supreme* empathy.

"The sentiment, maybe," said the ghost. "But the act did not affect you the way it would a normal person."

"Nonsense."

"And what about Mozo? Do you feel any shame for your second murder?"

He could not respond.

"How many times do you need to kill before you recognize you have a profound problem?"

Following Lita Fisher's rejection, he'd rented a studio apartment on 38th Street. A basement number with rodents and bugs and spiders. He'd named the spiders weaving webs in the corners of his windows, named them after women who'd cast him aside. The biggest, meanest of them, he called Lita. He caught flies with his hands and dropped them into Lita's web. How it tickled him to watch the spider descend on the panicked insects and paralyze them. He'd played this game for weeks. Then he'd gotten an assignment to drive a load of gumball machines to Denver and used the extra cash to move to a different building. He'd forgotten about his fascination with watching helpless creatures suffer.

He opened his eyes. The football game had gone into the fourth quarter. The Rams were trailing twenty-one to sixteen. He recognized none of the names on the jerseys. How long had he not been a part of society? He had trouble falling asleep again as he could not stop wondering, *Have I ever even belonged to the human race?*

Thirteen

The motel promised a Continental Breakfast. This always confused Blake, who figured a Continental Breakfast should be piping-hot pancakes, eggs, bacon, a cup of coffee, and a glass of orange juice. The name conjured an image of sterling silverware resting on a folded cloth napkin. The Sweet Dixie Inn's idea of a Continental Breakfast consisted of a stale, generic Danish and flat, burnt coffee in a Styrofoam cup. When Blake asked to settle his bill, the morning clerk, a large woman in wheezing, elastic pants said, "Murphy took care of that last night, didn't he?"

Blake said he'd put down a hundred-dollar deposit.

"Don't know nothing about that."

"How much is a room, normally?"

"Stay the whole night, should run you eighty dollars."

"That come with a lottery ticket?"

"There's other places you can flop."

Typical response in the twenty-first century—Business doesn't care about its customers? Business so goddamn corrupt it steals money from its customers? Oh well, too bad. Take your sorry ass somewhere else. In a country bursting with consumers, one person refusing to spend money in an establishment represented zero loss. Laziness. Lack of professional courtesy. Capitalism gone all wrong. As he walked to his car, he fantasized removing Crystal from the shoebox, marching right back into the lobby, and blasting a hole through the woman's pudgy face.

The ghost said, "You're going there awful fast these days."

"The hell are you talking about?"

"Murder."

Contempt for the motel's theft of his stolen money festered under his skin through Tennessee and into Kentucky. The emerald, rolling hills did little to quell his rage. He asked the ghost to tune the radio to some bluegrass. The ghost said, "And you think Ethan Hammond has a problem with clichés?" The radio landed on a right-wing station with a couple of Darwinists bemoaning the lack of progress on the Great Wall the rich guy in the White House promised. They spoke in accents less regional and more Ivy League, drawing the ends of their words as though sound slipped from their mouths at the speed of poured molasses:

"The president said Mexico would pay for it. You'd think the least he could do would be to send them a memo and let them know what's in store if they don't get their act together and write us a check."

The other man, his tone equally droll and arrogant, as though any disruption to the natural order of his immediate world would devastate on Pompei levels, said, "How many more illegals can this country handle? I was at Ruby's diner, over on 251, and darned if I didn't spot one in the kitchen, prepping the food. What in the world are they doing in small town America?"

Blake said to the ghost, "Silence would be better than this."

"Just don't want you to forget," said the ghost. "You walk between the shadows, outside the tribes."

The radio went silent as Blake crossed the Indiana state line and the Renault sputtered up 65 to Indianapolis. He hadn't seen his hometown in two years. The city's sparse skyline shimmering under a late afternoon sun induced nostalgia, an emotional infection he considered dangerous for its ability to trap one in a yearning for the impossible—a yearning for time travel, for erasing the wounds of aging. He remembered buying his first car in high school, a two-toned 1980 Chevy Caprice Classic. The owner said it'd been stolen and used in a liquor store holdup. His father didn't want him to, as he put it, waste money on material goods. What the hell else did one do with money? He paid the owner five-hundred bucks he'd amassed from delivering newspapers as a preteen and interning at Butler University, a job his father set up for him. He worked for a biology professor named Dr. McAbee who had him do curious tasks such as retrieving truckloads of cat cadavers for students to dissect and running those same cats, once split and gutted, to an animal cremation plant on the south side. The skyline had changed since those days. Market Square Arena and the Hoosier Dome no longer existed. How many concerts had he seen at MSA? He'd stand outside all day for general admission shows, dressed in the Midwesterner's headbanging uniform: jeans, black T-shirt, zip-up with the hood hanging over the back of a jeans jacket, and tennis shoes reeking worse than the rotting cats he drove to the cremation plant. Dio, Iron Maiden, Ozzy, he'd caught them all in their primes. By high school, he'd moved on to punk rock, preferring its untidy rage. He'd taken Lita Fisher to a DRI show in 1996. Before they entered the venue, she asked if she should remove the Star of David hanging around her neck. He suggested she cover it with her blouse's collar. Sure enough, neo-Nazis roamed the aisles looking for trouble. An entertaining riot broke out and no one, not even a minor army of Marion County sheriffs, could stop the band from playing and the kids from climbing stacks on both sides of the stage and diving from obscene heights. That venue closed following a GBH-led bill two weeks later in which three rows of seats were ripped out of the floor.

The good old days.

Blake embarked on his early sexual adventures in the back of that Chevy. Girls letting him kiss them, feel them up, and then slapping his hands when he tried to remove their pants. He'd eventually lost his virginity to the daughter of a secret service agent. He'd met her at a party on the Butler campus. She took him back to her parent's giant, *Eight is Enough* house in Carmel. He'd messed up before and told girls he'd never had sex and they'd cooled down, suggesting his first time should be with someone "super special." He kept his status as an innocent to himself and made love to the rich girl from Carmel. Lasted two minutes. Never felt better in his life. The girl said, afterward, "Maybe this isn't your night." He admitted, then, that he'd been a virgin; she accused him of lying and threw him out.

On the way to the front door, he saw her father, a behemoth yuppie schmuck sitting in a comforter watching a Cinemax import with two Italian women getting serious on a gondola. He wanted to tell the old man he'd just done to his daughter what the government had been doing to the people, a joke stolen from Woody Allen. The rich girl called him a few weeks later, asked him to come over, and told him a long story about how her cousin raped her on her fourteenth birthday. Then she told him to get lost. For the next couple of years, he treated subsequent girls the way she'd treated him—he fucked them once and never talked to them again.

The radio thundered to life with an AC/DC song on the classic rock station. The noise pulled him from his useless recollections. He got off at Pennsylvania Street and headed for the main library. He hadn't been there since high school, when his teachers matched him up with popular kids he despised for study projects. Inevitably, the goodie-two-shoes of the bunch would do all the work and complain about it after everyone in the group received the same grade. He liked the library's architecture, classical European, like the Louvre or other museums he'd seen pictures of in travel guides. A glass monstrosity with the aesthetic appeal of a translucent band-aid had been built onto the original structure sometime during the previous decade. He hadn't noticed when he drove for Yellow Cab because neither he nor his customers had need for a library. He found underground parking and took an elevator to the main atrium. A young woman in a black dress and a necklace with an upside-down cross nestled in her cleavage worked a circular information desk. Dimming sunlight splashed through an open ceiling supported by white arches. He approached the woman and said, "Do you still have the room with microfilm?"

The woman's head shifted on her neck as lines formed above her nose. "Microfilm?"

He mimed pulling a strip of microfilm from a reel and threading it in a reader. "You turn a crank, pages from newspapers roll by on a big screen."

"No idea what you're talking about." She seemed offended he'd asked her to be familiar with technology not invented that morning.

"I need to do some research. I need access to recent copies of *The Indianapolis Star*."

"You could probably find that online," she said. "The In…ter…net." She spoke slowly, perhaps having confused Blake for a senior citizen pre-dating the discovery of electricity. She directed him to a room in the old building with fine, oak tables and, mostly, empty bookshelves. Desktop PCs occupied the tables. The people clicking mouses and tapping keyboards wore rags and smelled like urine. He searched for an empty computer. Pornography occupied most of the screens in use, roided men and silicone women going at it in unnatural positions, sneering at each other as though they were making hate, not love. He found a place near the end. Dust particles swam in deep red beams bleeding through the windows from the day's dying sun. The computer required a library card number. He asked a woman next to him if there were any way to log on without one.

Tell-tale brownish injection scars dotted the veins on her frail hands. "I'm here to serve *you?*"

Blake searched for another librarian. He walked along a wall of paperback books to the room across the old building's main hallway. A man in a button-down shirt and red bowtie sat behind a wooden desk. He played a noisy video game on his smartphone. Blake said, "Excuse me, but I need to use the computers."

The man peered at him through thin, round spectacles. He offered the smarmy, didactic glare Blake's father donned any time he'd engaged him in a conversation about popular culture. A kind of dull, bored expression intended to denote the subject matter beneath him. In this case, he figured, the brittle man felt annoyed a plebian would ask him to do his job. "They're across the way, in the old periodicals room."

"Yes," said Blake. "I was just there. The computer asked for a library card number."

"That's correct." The man sighed and rested on his elbows, constantly glancing at his video game. Popping digital bubbles, obviously, of greater importance. "Do you have a library card?"

"Would I be talking to you right now if I did?" Blake had had enough. Had he become a *Get off my lawn!* kind of guy? Is that what being in your forties brought on? Librarians used to give a shit about patrons. Would the slightest mirage of kindness be too much? Did that make him an oppressor, asking someone else in the material world to take two seconds to crawl out of his self-absorbed skull and help another human being?

"*Well...*" The man snapped his head and faced the screen on his little electronic gadget once more. "This conversation is over."

Blake had never experienced such an abrupt dismissal by someone charged with, essentially, a customer service position. He imagined what sort of trouble he'd have gotten into had he treated passengers that poorly when he drove for Yellow Cab. He said, "Can I get a library card?"

Punctuating another sigh by dropping his shoulders and leaning back in his wooden chair hard enough to make it creak, the man said, "Do you have proof of residence?"

"I, ah, I don't know what that means."

The man's demeanor shifted. He must have thought he'd mistreated a bona fide imbecile and this faux pas wouldn't look good on his social virtue resume. "Oh dear," he said. "I apologize. Residence refers to the place you live." He enunciated slowly, the way morons addressed non-native English speakers because they believed comprehension depended on the speed at which words entered the ear. "So, like, a driver's license and a piece of mail, say, an Internet bill, something that shows you *live* here." He pointed to a window. "In Indianapolis. Do you understand?"

Resting on the desk with his fists, Blake said, "Now you listen here: what the hell sense would it make for me to use your goddamn Internet if I had my own goddamn Internet?"

"Sir..." The man's voice wobbled. "There's no need to get hostile."

"I've asked a simple question," said Blake, "and you've given me nothing but static. I'm going to ask you one more time, and then I'm going to give you a reason to be scared." As soon as he said it, he wished he hadn't.

"Do I need to call security?"

Blake raised his hands and retreated. No reason to summon undue attention. The rent-a-cops in the library might have been granted arresting powers. He backed away and found an elevator. As he descended to the parking garage, he watched two teenaged girls stare at their cell phones, oblivious to the world beyond their chiseled attention spans. He imagined pulling Crystal from inside his jacket and demanding the girls let him use their electronic gadgets to surf the Internet. Running his fingers along the bridge of his nose, he asked himself, "Where is all this coming from?" He could remember few times in his life rage hadn't dominated his emotional state. The woman from New Orleans, he suspected, had tamed him for a brief period. In her absence, the anger resurfaced.

"You didn't think twice about shooting the mayor of Raro Key," said the ghost.

"I thought they were blanks."

"That doesn't explain the ease with which you squeezed the trigger."

He paid for his parking at an automated machine. No rent-a-cops jumped from the shadows as he pulled out of the garage. The problem remained, however—where could one access older newspapers in the Grand Digital Age? Seemed the trouble he had tracking down information satisfied the desire of those in charge to make it difficult for individuals to form a coherent picture of current events. Like something out of *1984*, the only book his teachers in high school had forced him to read that he enjoyed. The poor sap in the novel, he couldn't remember the guy's name, worked for some agency where he erased or rearranged headlines and news stories. Turning everything digital had made it possible for such an occupation to exist in the real world. Things once expected, obvious, were questioned or denied online by people with no tether to the truth. In such an environment, would there be ethical consideration in altering history?

Pulling into a gas station combined with a McDonald's at Illinois and 38th, he parked at a pump and went inside to pay for a fill up. The woman behind the counter smirked when she saw him. The nametag on her gray uniform identified her as Tamara. She could have used a shirt one or two sizes larger as her short sleeves appeared to suffocate her arms. She said, "What do you need?"

Blake plopped down thirty bucks and said, "Number five."

"Sure thing." Tamara took the money and pushed buttons on the side of the register to free up the pump.

"I wonder," said Blake. "You know of any way somebody could use the Internet without having to have a membership card or cell phone or their own damn computer?"

She thought about it and said, "They got an Internet café in Broad Ripple. Just down the street from the Vogue. You know the area?"

He did. He told her so without explaining he'd driven a cab in Indianapolis for fifteen years. "I can just pay for a couple of minutes, they won't ask to see my ID or anything?"

Her mouth crumpled into a grimace. "You ain't looking at kiddie porn, are you?"

"No ma'am," said Blake.

"Yeah," she said. "I think they're cool."

He thanked her and returned to the pump to feed the Renault. The total came to just under twenty-seven dollars. He retrieved his change from Tamara and offered her two bucks. "For the info."

"We ain't supposed to take tips." She put the money in her breast pocket. "But it ain't like I'm getting paid enough to give a shit about the rules."

It took some time to find the Internet café in Broad Ripple. Tamara had been a bit confused about its precise location. It sat a block up from a Kroger's on Guilford in what appeared to be a private home. A yellow-bricked two-story house with amber trim on the windows and porch. A small sign posted on the lawn announced, *Netocracy!* No doubt a nod to democracy. They must have been optimists. Or naïve. Inside, a large living room connected to a dining room and a kitchen. Cubicles had been placed on the hardwood floor. Three people sat at them surfing the web. A flip-counter had been constructed in the doorway to the kitchen. A cash register and a mess of paper occupied it. Blake purchased a card for one hour's use of a computer. The young woman working the counter wore a paperclip through a piercing in the middle of her nose. She'd dyed her hair fire-engine red and decorated her black and white polka-dotted blouse with buttons celebrating her hatred of the current president. She took Blake's money and considered him with a cautious stare he noticed many young women regarded him with—had he been relieved of his "toxic masculinity"? Would he go crazy and shoot up the place with an automatic rifle?

After slipping the card into a reader on the side of a computer, he typed Gordon Lane's name into a search engine. Several pages of links appeared. He put them in order from most recent to the oldest. A headline from that morning revealed, INDIANAPOLIS AUTHOR HANGS SELF IN FLORIDA PRISON. Gordon Lane had, apparently, used his pants to fashion a noose and strung himself up in his cell. Real tidy. No need for a trial. No need for anyone to go looking any further into the assassination of the mayor of Raro Key. Had Blake not been the triggerman, he might have bought the story as easily as, apparently, every other idiot in the nation. He went back to the search results and opened an article from six months ago. Just an update—INDIANAPOLIS WRITER STILL IN COMA. Gordon Lane, it stated, remained in the ICU at Methodist Hospital. His next of kin, a man named Albert Hoffman, claimed medical expenses would drain the Lane fortune. He expressed relief that Gordon Lane's publisher, Ragnar Books, would release Gordon Lane's final, contracted work, *Destination Manifesto*. Blake would have to go to Methodist and see for himself whether Gordon Lane snoozed with a tube in his throat or if he'd woken up, made his way to Florida, and managed to get himself framed for murder.

With time still on his card, he chose to research a few other items. He typed in Sewell Harper and retrieved a handful of articles, including the pedophile's obituary. In the third article on the matter, he found his own picture, taken from his cabbie license. His fat, unshaven face, the puffy cheeks and donuts of blubber around his eyes…He didn't recognize himself, couldn't believe he'd ever occupied such a defeated husk of unhealthy flesh. The caption under the photo read, "Yellow Cab driver Lester Banks is wanted in connection with the shooting of a decorated public school teacher." Of course. After all he'd seen, why would he be surprised by the media's incompetence? The caption should have read: "Heroic cab driver shoots vile kiddie toucher in his disgusting face. Please send donations for legal services to…"

And then he remembered why he'd killed the pedophile. The girl, Chelsea Farmer. Pimped out and sold to a rich prick named Jerry Simon. He'd stolen Jerry's money and liberated the women held captive in his mansion. What had become of old Jerry? He entered the rich man's name and one article came back: PHILANTHROPIST DIES IN MOTEL FIRE. Mr. Simon, it appeared, had been in a rented room on the west side of town with two African-American prostitutes when a longtime resident in another room set fire to the building. Despite having eaten nothing since the Continental Breakfast at the Sweet Dixie Inn, Blake felt a weight form in his belly. Dental records identified the arsonist as Chelsea Farmer. She'd just turned 24, according to the article. Despondent, police suggested, of a severe addiction to drugs and, perhaps, depressed over the recent death of her mother, Ms. Farmer had doused her room with gasoline and set it ablaze.

He left the Internet Café without removing the card from the reader, without clearing his browsing history or even wiping out the Internet window he'd opened. He allowed himself to feel guilty about the death of Chelsea Farmer. He'd sold her to the rich prick, Jerry Simon. Mr. Simon had used heroin to control his stable of women. While Uncle Sewell had started Chelsea on the road to self-destruction, Blake had done nothing to help her find a different path. He had, in fact, given her a ride to, apparently, a few blocks shy of that road's morbid destination. She'd come to his room drunk and he'd slept with her. Not a good decision. He'd allowed a prostitute to talk him into pimping Chelsea out to perverts around the city. Not a good decision. He'd let a group of dirty cops rape her as a down payment for extortion they demanded to permit him to conduct business on their side of town. They'd dragged her up the stairs to a projection booth at a drive-in and violated her. And then he'd tried to escape his debt to the dirty cops by selling her to Jerry Simon. As he drove toward the hospital, the night lights of Indianapolis bounced psychedelic colors across the Renault's obscenely large windshield. He wanted to cry for Chelsea Farmer but found he could no longer engage in this most human display of grief.

He pulled into the short-term parking lot at Methodist and navigated corridors and waiting rooms. He found a general information desk, a circular number made of phony wood ringed with three levels of phony metal. He said, "ICU?"

The receptionist, her black scrubs complimenting her silver hair, tore her attention from her smartphone. She directed him to the appropriate bank of elevators. "Who you seeing?"

"An old friend." He walked away before she could ask anything else.

On the ride to the third floor, The Orioles crooned "Crying in the Chapel" through speakers embedded in the ceiling. An odd choice. Blake recognized it from *American Graffiti*, a movie he'd watched with his parents on television shortly before they split. He'd videotaped it and wore it out in junior high as he attempted to escape his mom and dad's screaming matches, to pretend he lived in a different era. His first experience with nostalgia, a nostalgia he couldn't possibly enjoy, having been born long after the time depicted in the film. He realized, on his own, yearning for the past produced nothing constructive in the present. He broke out of his self-pity in the eighth grade and started listening to Motörhead and Iron Maiden. Heavy metal helped him realize there were plenty of people like him, people who didn't give a shit about wearing golf shirts with stitched alligators or boat shoes or cheering like mindless lunatics at *Rocky* movies. The elevator dinged. He followed the receptionist's directions to the critical care ward. At a smaller desk outside two locked doors, a security guard stopped him. The man's ballcap barely contained an oval-shaped afro. He said, "Evening, chief."

Blake said, "I ain't in charge of a damn thing." He wanted to smack himself as soon as he said it. Herein lay the tragedy of his life—his inability to stop the wise cracks before they found air and offended their targets.

The man said, "That's very good, chief. What can I help you with?"

"I'm here to see an old friend of mine."

"Sure thing." The man clicked on a mouse and stared at a desktop screen in front of him. "Let's make sure your buddy's able to have visitors."

At that point, he could no longer stall. "I'm here to see Gordon Lane."

The security guard stopped looking at the computer. "Sorry, chief. Nobody here by that name." The man's prominent, bread-pan eyebrows traveled high on his forehead as he nodded, slowly, one time. A signal, Blake assumed, to drop the subject and leave.

A woman in burgundy scrubs joined Blake as he waited for the elevator. Far as he could tell, he'd gotten the answer he sought—something untoward had gone down. The feds, or someone worse, had made sure the security guard didn't let anyone snoop into the Gordon Lane story. He wanted to ask if the media had been around. Better to keep moving, though. The elevator arrived and he allowed the woman in scrubs to board before him. Her sleek, dark hair had been tied into a tidy bun at the back of her head. Her apple-scented shampoo filled the elevator as the doors closed. Between the second and first floor, the woman reached over and pressed the emergency stop. The lights in the elevator flashed and an electronic ping echoed around them. She stepped to Blake and cupped her hand at his ear. "They got Mr. Lane's room covered," she said. "Bad men. Serious suits. They wear sunglasses indoors, even at night. They got shit in their ears, you know, with wires crawling into the collars on their shirts."

"Mr. Lane is still here?"

She told him to keep his voice down. "They got microphones, cameras, everywhere. Shit don't happen in a hospital without official eyes peeking, official ears snooping, you know what I'm saying?" She didn't wait for him to acknowledge. "They moved in soon as the story broke on TV. Everybody knows it's bullshit. My homegirl Tiara, she spoke up yesterday. Said she's going to channel 13. Said she's going to set the record straight. Two more of them in suits, they come and take her away. Said they was with the government. Said they wanted to hear her story. I ain't heard from her since. Tiara, she's all over Twitter, even at work. She's posting shit twenty-four-seven. Nothing. Nobody's heard from her. Her boy Jayshaun, he's been blowing up my shit all day, looking for her."

"What about Gordon Lane's next of kin, this guy, Albert Hoffman? He been around?"

"Creepy dude. Looks like that dude on *The Munsters*. The dad, you know who I'm talking about?"

"Any idea where I can find him?"

She shook her head and depressed the emergency stop. The ping ceased and the elevator continued toward the first floor.

Blake said, "Hard to believe."

"What's that?"

"Folks think they can get away with this."

As the doors opened and the woman stepped off, she laughed and said, "Guess you got to the party late. Truth ain't got nothing to do with the twenty-first century. Not in this country."

He approached the exit. Two IMPD officers stood at attention. The one on the left, middle-aged, a blossoming pot belly stressing the lower buttons on his uniform's shirt, stepped to the side and smiled. "You have a good evening, sir."

Blake pushed past them. He didn't correct the officer for calling him sir. Technically, he *did* sign his paycheck.

Fourteen

Most of the motels in Indy refused to let Blake rent a room without seeing his identification. Even the joints with rodents hustling along the floorboards had computers on their dusty countertops connected to the Big System. He asked several clerks where he'd find an establishment whose management didn't believe every transaction must be documented. They gave him a variety of snarky answers. On the buzzing streets of Speedway, he found the Starlight, a crumbling, three-story motel. Looked like it might have been nicer in the early twentieth century, during the infancy of the Indy 500. As the race deteriorated into a show-me-your-titties fest, lodging around the track degenerated into crash pads for junkies, hookers, and others who'd given up on pleasing the Big System. Outsiders. Blake Ness's kind of people. He parked the Renault near the motel's crackling neon sign, blinking on and off, casting his car in alternating darkness and powder blue. Two women in Spandex and platform shoes shared a cigarette in the lobby, watching a mid-sized flat-screen television resting against the wall. An emaciated man in a flannel shirt spilling off his bony shoulders sat behind bulletproof glass. He said, "What do you want?"

"Ask me no questions." Blake palmed a hundred across the counter.

The man nodded. "You'll have to sign the register." He shoved a book with piss yellow, crusty pages under the window. "Police sometimes come around, want to see we're doing shit on the level."

He leaned closer and said, "How you sign it? Well, that's your business." Blake scribbled something resembling an EKG reading. The clerk pulled down a room key from a board mounted to his right. "Checkout's ten in the a.m."

Blake smiled at the women. He stuffed the key in his pocket and retrieved his shoebox and gym bag from the Renault. The clerk put him on the third floor. He'd have to conquer two flights of steps littered with people smoking weed and crack. The air smelled like gasoline. He held his breath and ignored the nagging pain in his knees as he climbed the stairs and found his room. Several people commented, some suggesting him too fancy for the Starlight. His unblemished skin must have offended them. Had he the energy to chat, he might have suggested they exchange their bad habits with good habits. A few simple exercises each morning. A walk through the produce aisle at the grocery store. Basic things everyone knew they should do but, for whatever reason, couldn't flip the switch in their minds to make the change. Didn't help they lived in a country that championed self-destruction. The combination of Puritanical impulses with prohibitive laws placing the most dangerous books on the highest shelves, tempting natural, human curiosity, had created a society in which self-loathing and masochism constituted rebellion.

He stepped into his room and turned on the light. A hole in the wall near a battered minifridge suggested rats might join him as the night progressed. Reminded him of his shithole apartment on the west side he'd lived in for over ten years before Chelsea Farmer knocked on his door and led him into the third and possibly final act of his life. Two small beds occupied the center. No attempt to doll them up, just basic, white sheets and felt blankets on top. Not even tucked in. Had they cleaned the room since the previous occupant? Blake lifted the covers on both beds to check for stains. He set the shoebox and gym bag on one bed and turned on the humpbacked television sitting crooked on top of the minifridge. He adjusted a set of broken antennae attached to a digital box and managed to secure channel 8. A woman with severe dimples and red hair delivered the latest complaint about the president. He'd written something offensive on Twitter. He'd said something nasty to a reporter. He'd failed to use environmentally-sound deodorant. Blake lay on the bed and half-dozed until the woman mentioned Gordon Lane, how he'd committed suicide in a Florida jail cell. The screen shuffled through different social media remarks by people Blake had never heard of, all congratulating Ragnar Books for refusing to publish Gordon Lane's latest diatribe. Nobody commenting on the book had read it. That didn't stop them from comparing it to *Mein Kampf*. The screen switched to a montage of people purchasing Gordon Lane's previous tome, *Breaking Glass*, and, at a different location, throwing it onto a bonfire fashioned from stacks of the bestseller. Blake didn't know too much about history, but he recalled a teacher telling him the Nazis had been keen on burning books. Odd that a man now accused of being one would have his work given the same treatment. All of it, the irony, the hypocrisy, made him think of *1984*, how corrupt governments controlled society through calculated inversions. When the picture returned to the woman with red hair, she said, "One less fascist in the world is always a good thing." He watched for her cheeks to flush at her own stupidity. It did not happen. The woman, apparently, peddled bullshit without the burden of shame. As he floated into a deep sleep, he imagined fucking the red-headed woman from behind, wrapping her hair around his knuckles and slamming into her hard enough to make her squeal.

Blake woke early and attended to his morning routine. He didn't bother looking for breakfast in the lobby. He found a chain restaurant serving veggie sandwiches and returned to the Internet café in Broad Ripple. On his way in, he thought little of the sky-blue Chevy Volt parked at the end of the block. Tinted windows barred him from peering inside, seeing who might be behind the wheel. He did, however, note the car's Virginia plates. He purchased a new card for the computers in the café, spent a few minutes tracking down Albert Hoffman's address, and walked back to his Renault. As soon as he took off, the Chevy followed him. He bobbed and weaved, zigged and zagged, until he no longer saw the Volt in the rearview mirror. *Virginia*. The CIA? At that point, why wouldn't the meanest cult in the country go after him? Had he given himself up at the hospital? No. He hadn't logged off at the Internet café the day before; whoever orchestrated the character assassination of Gordon Lane must have monitored searches entailing the author's name. He'd made it easy for them. He escaped Broad Ripple on Riverview and turned right on Kessler to head toward the west side of town. Albert Hoffman, according to his research, lived near 31st and Clifton. With the CIA possibly on to him, he decided to park several blocks away from his destination, a trick he'd learned when he drove for Yellow Cab. Dope dealers and dope users would hire him to drive them to sketchy locations. They'd have him wait around the corner. This allowed them, on foot, to gauge whether cops might be lurking. Police could pull over a vehicle and investigate. Not so easy with a pedestrian.

Most of the houses in the area had been refurbished. One and two-story colonial homes. The owners painted them a variety of pastel shades. Young people hanging out in the street gave Blake static, constantly asking him, "What you doing up in this neighborhood?" He kept his hand inside his jacket, near Crystal.

He found the address the sleuth site on the Internet claimed Albert Hoffman resided at, a corn-colored one-story rundown shack surrounded by a chain-link fence. Three Dobermans patrolling the yard salivated when Blake tried to open the front gate. An alarm went off, a wailing akin to a bomb siren, and the sleek dogs went ballistic. A window opened and a man who sounded as though he should have hosted *Masterpiece Theater* said, "Hush, already!" The dogs and the alarm simmered and the man behind the window said, "Who are you?"

"Name's Blake Ness. I wanted to speak with an Albert Hoffman about Gordon Lane."

"Who are you with?"

"Nobody."

"Is this a setup?"

"No sir," said Blake.

"You with the press?"

"No sir. I happen to know Gordon Lane had nothing to do with the assassination of the mayor of Raro Key."

The window slammed shut. Blake thought the man had heard enough and gone back to whatever he'd been doing before the alarm sounded. The dogs must have come to the same conclusion. They resumed their maniacal barking and growling until the front door to the house opened and a man taller than the doorway poked his head out and cussed at the hounds. His refined accent suggested he'd grown up in the New England area. Not the streets of Boston, rather, the outlying regions, the haunted landscapes of old American money. He wore a velvet bathrobe and leather slippers. He carried a pump shotgun over his shoulder and hustled the dogs into a garage to the left painted the same shade of yellow as the house. Once he'd secured the dogs, he opened the gate. "Hurry," he said. "They're going to erase us all."

Blake asked what he meant by 'us.'

"Anyone who knows the truth about Gordon Lane must be silenced." He led Blake into his home.

The place reeked of unkempt dog. Newspapers covered the floor of the kitchen, dining, and living rooms. An upright piano sat in one corner of the living room and a mustard-colored couch took up the opposite wall. A strand of wire, something appropriate for a fuse on a bomb, lined the floors, just above the baseboards. Blake said, "You're Albert Hoffman?"

"Naturally." The giant man offered Blake something to drink.

"No thanks."

Albert Hoffman pointed to the couch. "What is your connection to the mayor of Raro Key?"

Taking a whiff of the couch before sitting on it, Blake said, "In the interest of both of us being completely honest, I must confess, I'm the one who shot the geezer. That's how I know all this shit the news is saying about Gordon Lane is false."

"Fascinating." Albert Hoffman found a glass in the sink in the kitchen and filled it with tap water. He joined Blake in the living room, opting to sit on the piano seat, its legs wobbling as he made himself comfortable. "And what was your conflict with the mayor, if you don't mind my asking?"

"None," said Blake. "A man, a very wealthy, powerful man named Don Stinson gave me a choice. Said I could shoot the geezer or Don and his buddy Ethan Hammond or someone else working for him would help me commit suicide. Seemed like a no-brainer to me."

"Are you aware who Don Stinson is?"

"Beyond the fact that he lives in a castle, that he ruins children? No, not really."

The big man stood and disappeared down the hallway, his slippers crunching newspapers the entire time. When he returned, he handed him a paperback with a white cover and the word *Proof* stamped on it in red, fractured letters. Blake said, "Thanks. I don't read."

"That's Mr. Lane's final book." Albert Hoffman sat on the piano bench once more. "The book his publisher has just been compelled to cease plans for publication. Would you care to know what it's about?"

"A *Reader's Digest* summary would be excellent." Blake set the paperback on a wooden coffee table covered with survivalist magazines.

The dogs in the garage barked. Albert Hoffman listened. When the commotion subsided, he said, "First of all, you must understand Don Stinson's real name is Donald Lane. He is Gordon Lane's uncle. He attempted to molest Mr. Lane when Mr. Lane was in his early twenties. This should not have been a terribly traumatic event for Mr. Lane, but it inspired him to look into his uncle's activities, particularly when his uncle came into enough money to move down to Florida and purchase his own island. What Mr. Lane discovered was the fact that the most powerful people in this country and the world, for that matter, are involved, one way or another, in ritualistic pedophilia. It is, thus, not surprising to me that you are, for whatever reason, familiar with Don Stinson's treatment of young people."

The bomb raid siren howled again. The big man hoisted his shotgun under his arm and ducked into the kitchen. Blake followed him, keeping low. They peered over the top of a windowsill above the sink. Three men in denim jackets and jeans, their faces covered by red bandanas and sunglasses, climbed the fence and split up, two flanking the sides of the house while the first approached the front door. Blake pulled his .38. "Me and Crystal here can lend a helping slug."

"Let me show you something." Hoffman crouched and motioned for Blake to follow him. They crawled on the newspapers through the living room and down the hallway to a half bathroom. He lifted a fluffy, lime-colored bathmat, revealing a trap door cut into the tiled floor. "They used to run booze from here to the church on 30ᵗʰ Street during prohibition." He slipped his fingers inside a looped hatch and pulled it up, revealing an unlit tunnel below. "You scoot on out of here, now. I've got a marvelous surprise for these intruders."

"I can help," said Blake.

"Return to Florida," said the big man. "See to it Don Stinson doesn't get away with this, whatever it is he's attempting." He grabbed Blake by the back of his jacket and nudged him toward the narrow square in the floor. "Godspeed." He pushed him into the darkness. Blake tumbled a few feet and landed in a puddle. Rats screeched and scrambled. "Just feel your way until you see the lights of the chapel." And then the big man closed the door, sealing Blake Ness in darkness.

Blake searched the soft walls around him for a ladder. He found none. Above, gunshots cracked and thundered. He stumbled in the opposite direction, feeling the confines of the tunnel, his imagination fueled by the pitch-black void in front of him. He occasionally tripped over soft, warm animals hissing at him as he made his way back to his feet. Had the big man tricked him? Had he been working for the wicked ones? An explosion rocked the tunnel and the path behind him caved. He ran faster. A chorus of emergency vehicles racing to Albert Hoffman's neighborhood pierced the underground in muffled, sing-song waves. A pattern of blue, yellow, red, and green shimmered in the distance. He convinced himself he would suffocate if he didn't reach the end of the tunnel soon. He found himself looking up at another trap door with quarter-sized holes drilled into it. He jumped, tried to punch it open. His palm grazed the wooden hatch, rattling its hinges. It had been secured with a latch or a lock, he couldn't be sure. He called for help. His yells morphed into hoarse screams as he pictured himself dying there, underground, rats robbing worms of their rightful feast. Soft footsteps landed on the ground above him. Someone fiddled with the door and a multi-colored blaze flooded the abyss. Blake's eyes adjusted to the holy sight of a woman's hand reaching down, offering to help him to the surface. He sprang upwards and let the woman grab him by the seat of his pants as he squirmed onto the black and white-checkered tiles of the nave of the church. He rolled onto his back and caught his breath while the woman closed the hatch. Sunshine angling through stained-glass Bible scenes warmed him, made him appreciate the beauty of the *idea* of sanctity, safety. As he tried making his way to his feet, he slipped several times before catching hold of a pew and hoisting himself upright. Sturdy, pale plastic covered half the woman's face and she wore a basic, knit shawl across a demure, cream-colored dress. The skin on her left side appeared to have been barbecued. He wanted to ask how she'd been injured. He said, "Thank you. Thank you so much."

The visible features of the woman's face retreated, as though she'd confused him for someone who'd hurt her once, perhaps the very person responsible for her deformed state. When she spoke, she forced words through teeth and lips barely able to move. "There's been a terrible accident." She pointed toward the altar. Past it, Blake assumed. The direction of Albert Hoffman's house.

He started for two, arched wooden doors at the rear of the church. "I've got to get. Whoever's responsible, they're probably coming for me." He stopped. No reason to tell the woman more than she needed to know.

She said, "You can stay here. Evil cannot penetrate these walls."

Blake slowed. Underneath the stress and pain sitting on the woman's voice, he recognized pure tones of concern. A kind of music suppressed by the madness beyond the solace of the church. He watched her switch a keychain from one hand to another. The tiny, plastic, 1950s jukebox attached to it appeared to have been melted. A thin, red button remained intact. He asked her if it still worked. She smiled and pressed the button. Bill Haley and the Comets rocked around the clock through the most miniscule of speakers. Blake nodded. He said, "Nice." He opened the doors and the sun blinded him. He cupped his hand over his eyes and wished the woman well.

"I'll pray for you," she said as she floated back inside and allowed the doors to close on their own.

Helicopters hovered over a dark, swirling plume of smoke rising above Albert Hoffman's neighborhood. Blake walked to the end of a manicured lawn bordering the church. He figured out where he'd parked and headed in that direction. More sirens swept through the area like spirits winding between houses and businesses, letting the world know something awful had happened. A channel 13 van sped by, the reporter in the passenger seat adjusting his tie, as though it were the most important thing he would attend to that day. Why bother? Blake imagined pulling Crystal from his jacket and shooting at the tires. The van would flip into a public park across the way with playground swings half-hanging on lone chains, crooked basketball hoops, the nets tattered, so gray they might have been there since the last century. It had not rained while he'd been in town and yet, on the basketball court, puddles from a past downpour buzzed with mosquitos. Yes, what would the almighty media representatives think as the van rolled and smashed into the concrete bunker housing restrooms Blake assumed plagued by the permanent stench of urine and feces? He'd drag the reporter from the van and shove his face down a filthy toilet and ask, "Why bother? You're not going to tell anyone the truth, so why...the hell...bother?"

Blake shook his head, as though the seeds of rage responsible for the increasing number of violent fantasies running through his mind might spill out his nose and ears, as though the urge to kill, the inherent delight in taking lives had not set roots the day he shot the pedophile Sewell Harper. He'd coasted on rationalization since then, told himself cutting down a kiddie-toucher ranked highest on the list of excuses for homicide. He'd imagined going to the generic version of heaven, the city in the clouds seen in cartoons and Hallmark cards. He'd walk through the gates, accept St. Peter's congratulations for slaughtering a slaughterer of innocence. He'd sit next to God, discuss the parts of his life he hadn't enjoyed. He'd compliment the Grand Creator for the few moments of rapture, the moments of bliss with women, women he loved, women he lusted after, women he believed he understood, women who vexed him to the very end. He would ask why he'd been instilled with the notion that he would meet the girl of his dreams in his adolescence. Marry her. Make babies. Live a comfortable life behind a picket fence. As America had promised. Why, instead, had God made him an outsider, an angry individual in a sea of conformists? Why every time he turned on a television or went to the movies, phony men and women in Hollywood pointed fingers at him, blamed him for everything from the asteroid that killed the dinosaurs to the toxins in the air blasting holes in the ozone and baking the Earth. Why these morons called him "privileged," insisted he somehow rotated the cogs of the world against everyone but himself when, in fact, his entire life, the Big System bent him over every chance it got.

He found the Renault. He drove a block away from the chaos unfolding outside Albert Hoffman's. The explosion, it appeared, left houses on both sides in flames. Firefighters struggled with hoses to douse the crackling demon while families gathered beyond clustered emergency vehicles, many grabbing their mouths in horror, as though they couldn't believe tragedy like this could happen in their quiet, tiny square on the planet, as though dope dealing and drive-by shootings bookended the parameters of pain they'd been assigned. Blake slithered through side streets until he found himself on Tibbs, approaching a motel with a semi-truck-littered parking lot. Beyond that, four drive-in movie screens towered over the trees. Wicked cops collected bribes at a picnic table next to the snack bar and projection booth. Blake knew this because he'd paid them off for a week's work of pimping, two years previous. A deeper memory nagged, however, one of taking Lita Fisher to see a Batman movie there in a summer that seemed to belong to an entirely different lifetime. He'd made love to her in the backseat of his Caprice Classic, believed, as any naïve young man is apt to do, that watching her determined face beneath faded starlight produced a level of happiness he'd never lose. He'd believed they would marry and the prescribed middle-class routine would follow. When Lita Fisher wed a man who'd negotiated the necessary hoops to be what the masses perceived as successful, any attachment to hope vanished. His mother had abandoned him. His father had thrown him out. Then, the woman he *knew* he loved and would always love had shut the door on him in favor of material comfort. She'd even admitted it, telling him, "You'll never be the corporate type. How do you expect to afford the things I want?" He'd sunk in a quicksand of cynicism and nihilism, spent twenty years feeling sorry for himself. Now, however, he wished he could thank her for being honest. *Of course* she wanted a man who made money. Putting food on the table and keeping a roof overhead took effort. Living up the Great American Splurge, spreading one's arms and gathering in all the gadgets and doodads commercials on TV and the Internet and magazines insisted completed your life required discipline Blake hadn't possessed in his late teens and early twenties. Not until his mid-life crisis had he decided to get his shit together. And as he swerved into the exit lane of the drive-in, not knowing what drew him there, he understood, for the first time, his obsession with Chelsea Farmer, his attraction to her, had been an attempt to repair mistakes he'd made with Lita Fisher, two decades earlier.

As he passed under the first screen, he gleaned what he'd come to do: He wanted to put bullets into the police officers who'd raped Chelsea Farmer. He would pick them off like a child with a pellet gun at an old county fair, snapping wooden ducks in two, right down the line. Except, when he parked at the snack bar, only one squad car idled near the restrooms. He got out and approached the picnic table the corrupt pigs had previously occupied. A woman in uniform, roughly his age, sipped from a Starbucks cup. She'd set out playing cards in what appeared to be a game of solitaire. Her eyes thinned as she faced him and negotiated the sun at the same time. She'd removed her cap. Rebellious strands of her hair, obviously once tied into a bun, spilled in different directions. Blake imagined she didn't look too different after a vigorous night in bed. She must have understood where his mind had traveled. She smirked and raised a tisk-tisk finger. She said, "If ever I've seen a man on the edge of the world."

"Where are the guys who usually work this side of town?"

"I run the west side now, understand?" She beckoned him

closer. "What sort of sin are you pushing?"

"None." Blake put his hand in his jacket, placed his finger around Crystal's trigger guard. "Just dropping by to see what's what."

"You lying to me?" The woman identified herself as Lt. Boon. She let her shoulders relax. The lack of trust in her eyes went nowhere. "I find out you're selling pills around here, running meth for the cartels, whatever, I'll have your legs broken and drop you in the White River, you feel me?"

Meet the new boss...

It should not have surprised nor concerned Blake that the corrupt cop replacing another corrupt cop happened to be a woman. Society had trained him to believe women were morally superior. Women in charge? Surely, they couldn't stoop to the depths in which their male colleagues wallowed. He said, "I don't even live in this town."

The woman gathered her playing cards together and shuffled them. She cut them and shuffled them again. Then she fanned the deck and told Blake to pick a pair. "Just tap them, one, two. Real simple."

He did as she asked.

She pulled out the cards he selected and dropped them on the picnic table, face up. The ace and eight of spades. "Don't look so glum," said the woman. "The eight suggests you believe you are, in some way, trapped, helpless. The ace, however, negates that. The ace tells us you have an opportunity to squash whatever it is you think holds oppressive power over you and/or anyone else you're concerned about."

Blake nodded. "That's neat." He gripped the gun harder. "You milk the dope-dealers and pimps now?"

"That's a gauche way of putting it," she said. "Indianapolis, like any major metropolitan area, doesn't function without vice. I'm here to make sure it's all on the level. The vendors give up a percentage in exchange for operating without the threat of legal ramifications. In purely economic terms, it's business as usual."

"And if someone doesn't pay on time?"

Smiling, she said, "I break their fucking legs." Behind her, the pigs who'd raped Chelsea Farmer materialized, like ghosts. Loony, the biggest, fattest of them all, carried the other four in his arms, like a father presenting his babies to an unseen god for a brutal sacrifice. Maybe they'd come to accommodate Blake's imagination. Maybe he needed to see them, physically, to understand what he did next:

He pulled Crystal from his pocket and aimed at the cop's face. "This isn't about you." He squeezed the trigger three times, caving the woman's skull and sending her body into the wall of the snack bar and to the ground. She lay still, slumped over a black, industrial rat trap.

Fifteen

Blake tuned the television in his motel room to the local Fox channel. A fabricated blonde showing off her thighs in a banana-colored one-piece read from a teleprompter, the words dripping off her lacquered lips in a tone both sultry and condescending. Blake imagined bending her over the glass desk she sat at, hiking her skirt above her hips, and giving it to her with savage glee. He shook his head, hoped the old fury, the old rage would return to the cellar of his mind and stay put. His initial plan, after shooting the police officer, had been to hightail it to Texas and cross the border into Mexico. Figuring he'd never return to the States, much less Indianapolis, he swung by the one-story he'd grown up in on Capitol Avenue. It looked like a gingerbread house, so tiny. He couldn't believe there'd been a time he'd gazed at the pointed roof over the door and considered it an arrow, pointing to heaven, promising great things would happen once he became an adult and took on the world. The current owners of the house had let it go—mortar holding Sienna bricks in place had chipped and hollowed. He considered reprimanding whomever might be home. The front door opened, however, and a young father emerged with a boy, his son, Blake assumed, and a bicycle, a starter-bicycle. An unfamiliar brand. He'd ridden a Schwinn Stingray. His father felt training wheels created unrealistic expectations and removed them. He'd walked Blake and the bike to Butler University, put him on the bike's ruby banana seat, and shoved him down the steep, twisting road to Holcomb Gardens. He'd crashed three times before instinct took over and he figured out how to pedal, brake, and steer. The man living in the house now had not taken the training wheels off his son's bike. He'd dressed the boy in jeans and a long-sleeve shirt. The boy wore a helmet and elbow and knee pads. The father put his son on the bicycle and gripped the back of the seat as he implored the kid to pedal. Somehow, the boy managed to direct the bike into a tree. Blake had heard people his age disparage younger generations for not being tough. As though it were their fault their parents doted on them like fragile pieces of china. The coddling of the youth had only gotten worse over the last three decades. In time, people would roll through public places in giant, plastic gerbil balls designed to keep them safe from absolutely everything. The ghost told him, "If the masses call this progress, what can you do?"

He put the Renault in gear and attempted to peel out. The car sputtered and spit black smoke from the exhaust pipe. He took I-70 to I-57. Wandered New Madrid until he found a ranch house with collapsing aluminum siding and seven crappy cars on the overgrown lawn. Prices had been written on torn pieces of cardboard propped in their windshields. He wanted to ditch the Renault and lose whoever'd been driving the sky-blue Volt. A bone-skinny man calling himself Petey Whiplash, dressed in overalls and an oil-stained T-shirt, greeted him. Blake asked how much to switch out the Renault for one of the shitheaps. "Just a straight sale. You put whatever you want on the title so you don't have to pay too much tax on it."

Petey Whiplash said, "Boy, you think I pay taxes?" He patted a holstered Glock on his unnecessary belt and said, "Uncle Sam wants to snoop in my business, I got a clip full of complaints just itching for his attention."

Blake examined the engines on the vehicles. Two pre-1970 Chevys were missing cables on the carburetors. A 1980 Dodge Aspen, which looked pretty good on the outside—recently washed, original seaweed green paint maintained—had no battery or coolant. He settled on a 1988 Buick Skylark Petey described as "ornery" when pushed over fifty-five miles an hour. "It'll get you where you need to be," he said. "Just going to take a while longer to get there."

Blake gave him a grand and drove off, the monster choking and coughing on the way to the interstate. Once he forced the engine to do some work, the tempo evened and the car floated at a comfortable fifty-eight miles an hour. The lock on the trunk had been busted, so he kept his gym bag and shoebox up front. The radio worked. He listened to preachers offer advice to the wicked clear into Memphis before finding a motel called Better Than Nothing. He would have continued on to Texas and then Mexico, had the painted woman on the Fox channel not announced, "Florida's governor race is officially underway. Sarasota businessman and philanthropist Donald Stinson threw his hat into the ring last night at a fundraiser in Bonita Springs."

The picture cut to a ballroom filled with relics in tuxedos and evening gowns, clinking crystal glasses and fanning themselves with decaying hands. Don Stinson, dressed for a funeral, spoke at a glass podium: "It's time to send a message to the fascist in the White House. Florida's had enough. Say it with me…" He raised one arm, directing the audience, *Florida's had enough, Florida's had enough, Florida's had enough…*

The woman reading the news appeared once more and said, "Stinson is a registered Republican and has been quoted numerous times on his opinion that the party is moving in the wrong direction under the current administration." Either he meant the bald guy running Florida, the guy who looked like an anorexic Lex Luther, or the rich man in the White House. While he had a point, with respect to the Republican party, Blake could not allow him to vie for office. The man had orchestrated the quelling of Gordon Lane's book, it now seemed obvious, to avoid pesky questions from the press, such as:

"Sir, is it true you tried to cork your nephew?"

A dying ember of reason begged Blake to track down a copy of the book, read it, find out for himself what it said. This nagging demanded he force his way into the ICU in Indianapolis and convince himself Gordon Lane lived, even if in a coma. But he'd seen the activities in Don Stinson's castle. Nothing he'd witnessed suggested the people in Indianapolis lied to him. Soon, the plug would be pulled on Gordon Lane and no one would be able to stop Don Stinson. Suppose he won the position of governor, where would he go from there? The ghost showed up, sided with the flailing corpse of a conscience tied to a hive mind Blake had dismissed his entire life— "Are you going to risk your own freedom? The Don Stinsons of the world get what they want. Always have. Always will."

Blake thought of every tyrant in history, every yuppie scumbag he'd ever witnessed trampling the doomed without apology. He pictured a giant boulder, steamrolling little people who couldn't defend themselves, tumbling down through the ages. And Don Stinson wanted more than he already had? Maybe some headshrinker would find excuses in Blake's biography to snuff his passion for cosmic justice. No matter. He said to the ghost, "Sorry, bubba, but it looks like I'm headed back to Florida."

He entered the state from the west and cut off a chunk of the endless drive down 75. Time passed faster as he kept watch for law enforcement. He crept in the far-right lane and made sure to hold the wheel straight anytime a marked SUV passed. A few prowlers lurked in the middle of the road, officers no doubt requiring either a nap or a boost to their ticket-writing quotas for the month. None seemed interested as his Buick wheezed by like an old person searching for a single, pure breath. The sun baked the interior, forced him to roll down both the driver and passenger side windows. Steamed air slapped him, battered his eardrums. The ghost tuned the radio again and again, never affecting Blake since he heard nothing but the furious wind.

He gassed up outside Tampa and arrived in Raro Key as the sun set and a gulf breeze cooled the land. A flock of emergency vehicles flanked Lonesome Cowboy Bill's, lights spinning at a casual pace, painting temporary streaks across the arch's stucco exterior. Blake pulled into the lot and parked amidst a cluster of microvans. He removed the gun from the shoebox, stuffed it down the front of his pants, and placed the gym bag on top of the shoebox. No telling who might be waiting for him. He locked the car and moseyed toward the ambulance and fire trucks. Two deputy sheriff squad cars bookended the other vehicles. A minor crowd near the arch backed up as paramedics in navy coveralls wheeled out a stretcher. They'd arranged the mangled, lifeless body of the young woman with Tinker Bell dreads in a position making it look as though she were running, her legs crooked and mauled, bone fragments shooting through slimy, crimson gore. Not nearly as bad, however, as the chunk taken from her upper torso, from half her breast clear to her arm, which had been placed next to her like an unattached piece of a jigsaw puzzle. Her friends, all marked with the scorpion tattoo near their belly buttons, followed the paramedics so close an officer had to tell them to back off.

Blake turned to a young man with his hair tied in a snake coil on the top of his head. From five feet away, he could smell the young man's aversion to soap. He kept his distance as he spoke. "Shark?"

"Lalo, bruh," said the young man. "Wallace ain't getting paid to bring sheep no more. Lalo decided to take a pound of our flesh instead."

"That's a skinny girl," said Blake, "but I think the alligator took a lot more than a pound."

"That a joke?"

Blake didn't know how to tell the young man he'd divorced himself from guilt. He certainly couldn't say, "Bubba, I've killed three people and I don't feel a goddamn thing." The ghost asked whether this made him proud. "You trying to shame me?" said Blake.

"If you don't feel shame, why would my intentions matter?"

"If you know I don't feel shame, why would you start the conversation in the first place?"

The young man shook his head as he walked away. "Bruh," he said, "you're crazy."

The ghost said, "I guess there's no fooling you." To whom he spoke, Blake didn't know.

One of the deputy sheriffs glared at him. "You talking to me?" she said. Blake nodded to the slender woman and started for the businesses across the street. No lights shone from the establishments. Too early for the diner or massage parlor to be closed. As he approached the other side of the road, identical orange stickers pasted to the doors of each shop revealed themselves—giant, black stenciled letters announced, SEIZED! Though the fine print wouldn't make a difference, he took a closer look at the sign posted on the door to the massage parlor. Unpaid taxes, apparently, the cause. One of those technicalities the brutal hypocrites in charge employed anytime they didn't have the guts to meet their enemies with rolled sleeves and bare knuckles. How long would such a process take in the normal world? Legal action, even the kind punishing the poor and making the wicked salivate like rabid dogs, took at least several weeks to snail through labyrinths of ink and rubber stamps. And yet, Mozo had died only a few days ago and the thriving capitalists of Raro Key had been given the official boot. Whomever had locked up the massage parlor had stored a half-dozen female mannequins dressed in bikinis in the lobby. He peeked into Trascendente, whose sign had already been removed. The counter and the shelves no longer existed. Nothing but two stone statues of panthers the size of Dobermans occupied the dust-covered floor. Spiderwebs fashioned from material thick as rope filled the diner. Rats and mice squirmed in cocoons fashioned by whatever arachnids had spun the webs. In the record shop, only the pedestal with the record player on it remained. The old suitcase model had been replaced with a plastic-shelled Mickey Mouse unit. A record spun on the turntable. It must have been scratched as the needle hopped on the same phrase, over and over:

death of us, death of us, death of us…

His stomach folded. He felt the urge to vomit, but only dry-heaved. He rounded the corner and climbed the fire escape. His knees ached. "Quiet," he said to the pain. No locks had been placed on the door leading to the apartments. He entered his room. The radio sat on top of the dresser and the sheets on the bed looked as though they hadn't moved one way or another since the last night he'd slept there. Then he heard Linda Lee's voice booming through the walls. He stepped into the hallway and tracked the sound to Mina's apartment. He nudged the door, peeked inside. Empty, aside from the same furniture from his room and, for whatever reason, Mina's television, propped on the dresser and left running.

On the TV, Linda Lee, wearing a gold, strapless top, sat behind her canary desk with her usual dour expression, her high, round cheeks collapsing in sighs of disapproval every few seconds as she conveyed a sordid tale of sex and casting decisions made in the film industry, how women in the movies had had enough of wart-covered dragon toads forcing them to sleep with them for work. Not a bad development in history, far as Blake could tell. The entertainment business had long been a refuge for men who couldn't get laid in the normal, nine-to-five world. They occupied dark, shady offices, shuffled numbers on paper like they meant something, convincing naïve little girls from Nebraska to open their legs for a taste of fame. Unfair all around. Blake hoped the women in Hollywood had the money and power to crucify the bastards.

Power.

His grandfather's word. Again. Except, perhaps, power concentrated in hands his grandfather might never have imagined. Linda Lee had power. He said to the ghost, "Maybe she can help."

To which the ghost said, "You're a little old to be doing your mainframe thinking with your gonads."

To which Blake said nothing.

He crossed the bridge to Sarasota. He parked downtown and searched for information on Linda Lee. An old couple walking a pair of retrievers said she'd been known to frequent The Exchange, a bar in which the city's minor population of the young and affluent sought one-night stands. Quick research along Main Street revealed The Exchange occupied the third story of a pastel, art deco building with a movie theater on the first floor. No sign announced its location. Several women in smart office skirts and blouses, seated at a sidewalk café serving lattes and New York-style pizza, explained the winding steps on the side of the building led to the only door to the club. A woman with Droopy-like jowls said, "You'll need to level-up your wardrobe." She suggested a jacket and tie, and not "some garbage" from a box store. "Best bet is Jos A. Bank." She told him how to get there. Then she said, "Be prepared to bribe the gorilla at the gate."

"Of the clothing store?"

"The club." She and her friends sipped their coffee drinks and smiled, their eyes slim, twinkling with mischief, as though they didn't believe for a second Blake Ness would work his way into The Exchange.

But he did. He disguised himself with khaki pants, slick, leather shoes, an Oxford shirt, a simple red and blue tie, and a sportscoat costing four hundred bucks. He wanted to put the outfit on in the fitting room and climb out of the building through the ceiling. Giving up all that dough for threads that felt like a full-body straight-jacket…As he tightened the tie around his neck, the ghost said to him, "Not too different from the way they snuffed me, eh?"

He dropped a heap of cash and returned to The Exchange and parked. People dressed like the wealthy snobs who'd snubbed him his entire life climbed the iron staircase. Blake made the hike up the steps, his knees begging him not to, and tried to blend in with a group of three couples smothered in perfume and cologne. The women at the café had described the doorman accurately: Nearly seven feet tall and half as wide, his hairline had receded enough to reveal a bulbous forehead jutting beyond the longitude of the rest of his face. The name Abraham had been stenciled on a gold tag attached to the breast pocket of his tuxedo. He dropped a paw the size of a frying pan on Blake's shoulder. "Not seen you before, my friend."

"No fault of mine." He tried to jerk loose from the monster's grip.

The doorman squeezed, let Blake know snapping his shoulder blade into pieces presented no significant challenge. "You familiar with the pass phrase?"

"You didn't ask them for any goddamn pass phrase." He pointed at the couples who'd slid by without contest.

"I'm familiar with them. Not so much with you."

Did the gorilla work for Don Stinson? Blake didn't remember seeing him at the castle. He extracted a thin stack of bills from the fold of cash in his pocket. "What's it going to take to get you to shut up and get the hell out of my way?" He wanted to pull Crystal and blast a tunnel through the monster's skull.

"Excellent question." The doorman made calculations on his flabby fingers. "Of course, you've requested two services, so there needs to be two charges."

"Just get to it."

"A grand makes you a figment I've neither seen nor heard."

Blake slid ten bills into the gorilla's breast pocket, briefly snagging it on the pin holding the nametag to the jacket.

Thick, red candles spaced ten feet apart burned in copper plates attached to the walls. Aside from fluorescents posted over the bar, the candles provided the only light in the long, narrow room. Extra candles bordered a stage at the far end where a band consisting of a tuba, cello, and steel guitar produced music appropriate for Dali's funeral. The musicians wore sky-blue and white-striped pants and jackets and top hats slinking to the side, as though they'd crawled out of a Dr. Seuss book. The young crowd huddled in clusters, everyone cradling drinks and leaning forward to ask each other to repeat themselves. Blake stayed close to the wall, trying to scrutinize the women without freaking them out. A few noticed. Most scowled. He heard the refrain from an old Charlie Brown cartoon in which Snoopy got evicted wherever he went:

No dogs allowed.

As he crossed the front of the stage, covering his ears to taper the droll, syrupy music, he spotted Linda Lee at the end of the bar. She tapped a credit card on the counter and bobbed her head to the band's morphine rhythm. She'd changed from the outfit she'd worn on the air earlier, now shimmering under the joint's scant illumination in a black one-piece sprinkled with multi-colored glitter, the back plunging enough to allow a view of hips sculpted by, presumably, hours of squats in a local gym. She dropped her credit card and leaned over to pick it up. The front of her dress slipped and her right breast, unbound, nearly spilled out before she trapped it in the crook of her elbow and stood up. Blake closed the space between them.

"Evening," he said.

She turned to the bartender. Her perfume, a musky buttermilk scent Blake had never smelled before, must have been customized. She said to the bartender, "Fauna, can I get my mimosa already?"

Fauna, slim as a car antenna, snapped his fingers and pointed at her. His head tilted until it rested sideways on his shoulders. "Sit tight, girl."

"Listen," Blake said to her, "I'm not going to bullshit you. I got a story I think you need to look into."

Her dropped jaw emphasized an atomic sigh as her eyes marched a perfect circle. "Do I *look* like I'm at work?"

Blake said, "It's about Raro Key. The mayor, Mozo. The assassination."

Fauna landed a tall glass filled with molested orange juice in front of her. "WLVE's tab?" he said. She waved her hand at him, as though he were a fly buzzing in her ears. Fauna's skull pivoted on his neck as he mimicked her gesture and joined a barback restocking the ice bin.

Linda Lee said, "That's last week's news."

"It happened, what, four days ago?" said Blake.

She gulped from her drink and wiped her mouth, smudging her cherry lipstick, making her look like a child enjoying a glass of Kool-Aid. "Gordon Lane killed himself. Life goes on."

"You don't want to know the truth?"

"We already broadcast that."

"What?"

"The truth."

"No, you didn't."

She finished her mimosa with another gulp and slammed the glass on the bar. "You one of these retards who voted for Orange Hitler? You going to call me fake news?"

"What would you say," Blake stepped closer to her, "if I told you Gordon Lane didn't pull the trigger?"

Sixteen

Linda Lee lived in a bungalow on St. Armands, near the Pansy Bayou. Harsh, Spanish roof over unwashed white walls. Stucco border fence. Empty swimming pool a few feet from the ocean. Blake followed her in his car. She drove a smoke-colored Porsche 911, a model from the 1980s, the kind one could be seen in without embarrassment. As they walked up the twisting stone path to her front door, Blake said, "You must be rich."

"Not yet," she said.

The sterile order of the exterior did not prepare him for the interior, which had been crammed with art projects of various genres—sculptures made from trash, paintings assembled from magazine clippings. Placed in between the sculptures were couches, tables, and other furniture of different shades, as though they too had been plucked from dumpsters and sidewalks. She said, "Please," and pointed at a plush, flying saucer-shaped loveseat.

Blake struggled with the rounded back of the small couch before leaning forward and resting his elbows on his knees. Linda Lee stood over him, reminded him of being a child, when most authority figures in his life were women. Linda Lee asked if he wanted a drink. She nodded to a bar fashioned from a wagon wheel turned on its side. "No thanks," said Blake.

She squeezed in her lips and touched her chin. "Oh, are you sure?" She sounded like a mother coaxing an infant to eat Gerber goop. "Let me slip into something more productive." As she disappeared down a hallway whose walls had been decorated with newspaper print, she said, "You think about that drink, mister. I don't want you freezing up on me when you tell your story."

He promised her no such thing would happen. As he took in the various pieces of art—human forms made of hubcaps, an obvious nod to the Holocaust fashioned from chicken wire and mannequins dressed in stripes, and different unidentifiable creatures crafted from every species of trash Americans produced— he scolded himself for not being able to stay focused, for believing he could not take this woman seriously without first sleeping with her.

"If you let her seduce you," said the ghost, "she owns you."

"She'll *think* she does."

"This is too important."

She returned in a sheer, silk slip. She eased onto the loveseat next to him and crossed one leg over the other, hiking the slip high enough to reveal she wore nothing underneath. "Now, tell me again how you think you're Gordon Lane?"

Blake cleared his throat. "Gordon Lane is in a coma, a thousand miles up the road."

"Gordon Lane hanged himself in a jail cell on the mainland, right here in Sarasota. I covered it myself. I saw them wheel him out on a stretcher. I saw them drive him to the morgue."

"What did he look like?"

She shrugged. "They don't parade dead bodies like items at Macy's, you know. They had him under a sheet, out of respect."

"Ms. Lee…"

"Linda."

"Yes, Linda," said Blake. "*I* killed Mozo. *I* put the bullet in the mayor of Raro Key. I can take you to the very spot I shot him from."

"None of this makes sense." She placed the back of her hand against her forehead, like she had a migraine, then shook her shoulders and slapped her arms against her hips like a chicken. "Mr. Ness, I need a drink. I need you to drink with me so I don't feel like an alcoholic. Can you do that? Can you nurse a whiskey and Coke while I chug one down?" She stood and negotiated the space between the UFO couch and several coffee tables. She worked some bottles, glasses, and ice at a bar behind the loveseat. "You promised me a Pulitzer, back at the club. I sat in front of those cameras and assured the people the gods' honest truth was the Nazi Gordon Lane shot down Raro Key's beloved founder. You think they value redemption, the old farts who hand out awards?"

"Do you consider yourself a journalist?"

"For now."

Carbonated liquid cracked ice cubes.

"Then you should be concerned with telling the truth. The objective truth."

She returned and handed him a short, fat glass. "Southern Comfort."

"You don't have any Jack Daniel's?"

"This is a civilized house." She slid her pinky along her thigh, inching the bottom of her slip higher. "It's impossible to be objective, Mr. Ness."

"That's a way contemporary society rationalizes dishonesty and bias."

She frowned. "You sure you're not just a paranoid conspiracy theorist? You're not asking me to believe a madman, are you?"

"That's debatable," said the ghost.

"That's debatable," said Blake. "But I know I pulled the trigger. I was hired to do it. Hired, with my own money."

"Drink up, Mr. Ness." She demonstrated, took a swig from her own glass. "It's so humid, this time of year." She wiped sweat from the glass across her cheeks. "Even with air-conditioning, it's hard to cool it down. These days, especially."

Blake said, "You win." He sipped from his glass. The cola quelled the syrupy taste of the booze. He drank until the soda overpowered the liqueur.

She asked him to continue telling his story. "So far," she said, "I'm not convinced I should believe a word of it."

"You familiar with a guy named Don Stinson?"

Her back straightened. She clamped her lips together.

"I'll record that as a yes." Blake took another swig. "Don Stinson set me up. I couldn't refuse. Not if I wanted to keep breathing."

"Why would Don Stinson want Mozo dead?"

"Mozo, and Raro Key, for that matter, don't seem so important." He finished his drink and set the glass on a zig-zag-shaped coffee table made of plastic and painted to resemble lacquered wood. "Don Stinson's running for governor. He can't have anybody crawling out of the past with dirty stories about his fondness for fondling young folks."

She set her glass next to his. Despite the booze turning his brain to putty, he felt certain she'd lifted it to her mouth without actually drinking. She said, "I'm still not sure what you're driving at… How does the Nazi Gordon Lane fit into this?"

The ground tilted like an amusement park ride. Blake's voice slurred. "First of all, you got to stop with the Nazi shit. Far as I can tell, Gordon Lane never invaded Poland. Second, and most important, Gordon Lane is Don Stinson's nephew. Gordon Lane claims Don Stinson propositioned him once. His own goddamned nephew. He wrote about it in the book they just banned."

"They didn't *ban* it." She sounded like a Valley Girl. "It's, like, a private company. They can choose to publish what they want." Now she reminded him of the parrot at the bar. Mindless. Programmed.

He held on to the table for balance. He squinted to read the carved signature in it—*Lindsy Stinson*. "Who's this?" He pointed to the signature.

"You think Linda Lee's my real name?" She no longer sounded like an adult. "Do I *look* Korean?"

He scanned the room. The same signature adorned every piece of art. "So, you're…" His head slumped. The ceiling, for a moment, exchanged places with the floor.

Linda Lee moved closer. A wave of mint-infused booze-breath forced Blake to grimace. "Now you listen to me," she said, her voice almost a whisper. "Only thing I ever got for keeping my mouth shut about Mozo knocking up my mom was inheriting that stupid fucking island. It's mine now and I'm doing what Don Stinson, the man who took the time to raise me, told me to do. I'm selling it to Dolent Enterprises. I'll be damned if some looney tune from nowhere is going to shit on that." She waved her hand across her juvenile art projects. "You think I want to spend my life looking pretty for a TV camera? I have *real* dreams, get it?"

Blake wanted to argue with the woman, ask what would become of the alligator, of the kids on the beach, the girls in the massage parlor. He tried to speak, produced only wobbling syllables adding up to nothing. Linda Lee's thighs smacked him in the cheek as he tumbled onto her lap. He didn't pass out. Signals from his brain commanded his arms to move, but they refused. Linda Lee rolled him off her and let him crash into the coffee table before hitting the floor. He watched her from an angle as she dialed a number on her cell. She explained to whomever picked up the other end that she had lured and captured "a nuisance" who could "fuck up the whole thing."

The floor rolled like an unsettled ocean as Linda Lee shuffled through her house. She changed into sweatpants and a Greenpeace T-shirt and made food in the kitchen. Smelled like garlic and chicken, though Blake couldn't trust his senses. The woman returned with a steaming plate. She turned on a stereo somewhere Blake couldn't see and contemporary pop music, sounding even worse under the influence of whatever she'd slipped him, forced itself beyond his ears and into his head. The lyrics were flat, straightforward. Some kid mumbling about bending his true love over and smacking her ass. Linda Lee sat on the loveseat and rested her bare feet on Blake's shoulders. He tried to ask her if the drug would eventually kill him. Whatever he said, she insisted she didn't understand. She said, "Sit tight. Daddy will take care of you."

The meaning of this cleared when the goon brothers, Tweedle-Dee and Tweedle-Dum, arrived. Like hired movers, they picked up Blake and carried him out of the house. Again, signals from his brain demanded he squirm, kick, fight. These signals traveled like rockets through his bloodstream and fizzled as his nervous system refused to heed them. It must have made him heavier. The goons constantly stopped and adjusted their grips.

They lugged him across the winding, stone path outside Linda Lee's to their gold, sparkly SUV. Tweedle-Dum forced Blake into a headlock while he opened the back door. He hoisted him into the vehicle. Tweedle-Dee pushed the bottoms of Blake's feet. The halfwit brother slammed the door, shoving Blake's feet toward the floor. Hints of movement returned to his limbs. He took this as a sign the drug would not be fatal. He spent exhausting levels of energy crawling to an upright position. He patted his belly. If he had his revolver, he'd put bullets in the Tweedle brothers' skulls. But he'd left Crystal in his car, along with his money.

The goon brothers got in and, per usual, Tweedle-Dum drove. As the SUV pulled away from Linda Lee's, the sky-blue Chevy Volt with tinted windows snaked out from behind Blake's Buick and followed them. The goon brothers transported him to the mainland and across the shoreline to Don Stinson's island. Tweedle-Dee got out and punched the code for the gate on the bridge. The SUV rumbled over uneven planks and crunched gravel on the drive to the roundabout in front of the castle.

Tweedle-Dee opened the rear door and said, "You ready to walk on your own?"

Blake spilled out of the vehicle and onto the gravel. Whatever drug he'd been slipped, it must have included a painkiller. He felt nothing despite tiny gashes torn into his palms. He wiped his blood onto his pants. The goon brothers helped him to his feet. Each lodged a hand under an armpit and half carried, half dragged him inside the castle. The building's stone walls thumped from techno thundering in the basement. The goons forced him up the stairs, ignoring his pleas as his toes slammed into the steps. On the roof, Don Stinson, looking like a librarian in a beige, button-down shirt and yellow bowtie, stood to greet him. "Mr. Banks," he said. "I thought you would have been smart enough to leave the country. I guess not, guess not."

The goon brothers shoved Blake toward the table. He caught his breath and said, "I told you, Lester Banks no longer exists."

"Not according to the *Indianapolis Star*." The old pervert held up a recent edition of Indy's mainstream newspaper. Chubby, goofy, stupid Lester Banks, smirking for a photo he'd taken for one of his cabbie licenses stared back at him next to a headline: DECORATED IMPD OFFICER BECOMES SERIAL KILLER'S LATEST VICTIM.

"Who the hell thinks I'm a serial killer?" Blake looked for a place to sit. He reached for an iron chair tipped on two legs against a wall. Tweedle-Dum wrapped his battery-sized fingers around his collar and threw him to the table. Blake addressed Don Stinson— "Look, I'm pretty sure you had your wife killed because Mozo knocked her up. I mean, it seems to me, you know… You shouldn't have had a wife in the first place."

Don Stinson's face flushed. His cheeks puffed as he bit his lip. "You weren't a problem before. But you are now. Definitely a problem now." He nodded at the goon brothers. "Fishy fishy time."

Tweedle-Dum pinned Blake's arms behind his head and shoved him through the blue door. He forced him down the spiral stairs. The annoying techno beat summoned a headache. In the party room, or whatever Don Stinson called it, a small collection of wealthy people in tuxedos and dinner dresses and masks over their eyes stood on the perimeter of the glass dance floor, ogling underaged boys and girls, all nude, dancing and writhing in sync with the alleged music. The fake Bible-thumper, Ethan Hammond, strutted out from behind the DJ booth. He tapped on the booth's plexiglass and snapped his fingers. The music reduced to a lone kick drum, over and over, like a broken record. A chain lowered from the darkness. A fresh, intact harness had been attached to it. Blake turned to flee and ran into Tweedle-Dum. The halfwit spun him around and flicked him to the center of the glass floor. Underneath, the tiger sharks snapped at each other. Blake tried crawling away. The goon brothers grabbed him by his arms and legs and lifted him. Ethan Hammond undid the leather restraints on the harness and motioned for the goon brothers to bring him over. They positioned him under the harness and forced him to keep still as Ethan secured his limbs in the separate restraints. He tightened them, made it impossible to escape. Blake stared at the water, at the hungry beasts swarming beneath him. He expected some revelation, perhaps his life flashing before his eyes. He only saw Ethan Hammond, gawking at him like a child promised a piece of candy. He strained to raise his head and speak to the cliché junkie: "I'm not jailbait, you sick fuck."

Ethan Hammond smirked as he removed his hunting knife from a sheath and placed the sharp side of the blade against Blake's neck. "Say hello to the devil for me."

Two ear-piercing pops disrupted the repulsive drumbeat pounding the speakers. All other noise died. Even the sharks calmed for a moment. Ethan Hammond, the naked children with scorpions sketched onto their flesh, and the rich people gathering at the edge of the glass to watch the slaughter looked at each other, looked over their shoulders, all trying to fathom who'd set off fireworks. Only the goon brothers remained still. Blake compelled his body to swing to the left as Tweedle-Dum collapsed. His brother landed on top of him. They faced the ceiling. Blood trickled around bullet holes in their foreheads, leaked onto the glass and, it appeared, seeped through cracks where the pentagram separated. Ethan Hammond dropped his knife and ran for cover. Another high-pitched crackle and Bible Boy smacked the floor, holding a fresh wound in his calf.

The crowd separated for a diminutive, female form walking into the indigo light. Blake believed, for a moment, he'd been saved. His chest sank inward as he realized the woman from New Orleans, Felicia Hill, a woman he should never have taken for granted, had tracked him down. She'd worn her orange and white-striped, tighter than tight one-piece showing off her thighs. An outfit she knew Blake couldn't resist her in. She carried Crystal, his .38, in her hand. She kissed him on the cheek and said, "I told you to stay in Metairie, didn't I?"

Seventeen

She unfastened the restraints and let him fall. As his body crashed next to the goon brothers, the glass pentagram screeched. Thin lines snaked from where he'd made contact. He jumped to his feet. "The floor's going to give." He tried to move Felicia toward the huddled crowd of rich people and naked teenagers. She refused to budge.

Ethan Hammond lunged for his knife. Felicia jabbed Crystal's barrel at his temple. "You stepping on my territory?" She waved the gun at Blake. "Only person's going to kill this piece of shit is me." She nodded at Blake. "A little help?" She prepared the restraints on the harness.

Ethan tried worming away. Blake locked his fingers on the skinny man's neck. "I only wish these kids weren't so doped up. They should do this for themselves." He forced Ethan's hands into the restraints. Felicia wrapped the leather around his wrists and tightened them. Blake kicked his legs from underneath him and held him in the air by a belt loop while Felicia secured his ankles. Blake walked to the DJ booth. The DJ had disappeared. Maybe he'd joined the crowd at the edge of the pentagram. He scanned the control panel, experimented with several knobs and levers until he found a long, slotted lever that dropped the harness and sent Ethan Hammond racing to the floor. Ethan's face smashed into the glass with a resonant crunch. Thicker cracks zig-zagged from where his skull landed. Blake pushed the lever forward and the harness raised into the air. He pulled it back, little by little, jerking the harness toward the ground. "I think I got it." He inched the lever upward and the harness took its time rising. "I think I don't care." He snapped the lever down. Ethan's face bounced off the dance floor. Blake pushed and pulled the lever with abandon. The layers of glass between Ethan and the sharks shrieked. Felicia and anyone else standing on the pentagram cleared out. Blake leaned over to a microphone between two digital turn tables and said, "Testing, testing." His voice boomed from the speakers. "Hey, Bible Boy," he said. "Any last prayers?" Ethan Hammond shouted something. Blake couldn't hear him. He throttled the lever for the harness until the glass exploded and disappeared. The goon brothers rolled into the pool and the sharks shredded them. Blood dimmed the blue lights in the water. Ethan Hammond screeched, reminded Blake of the sheep on the beach. The sharks swarmed him. He vanished in a crimson cloud.

The crowd dispersed, ran up the stairs screaming, cursing, vowing revenge. The chaos filled Blake with an excitement similar to the rush he'd felt watching spiders paralyze flies in their webs. He liked their fear. He liked that he'd been responsible for it. Felicia stood at the far end of the bloody pool. She called him over and traced Crystal's barrel from his forehead to his crotch. "I ransacked your car before these dorks kidnapped you. Had the car towed, just so you know. I'm disappointed you thought getting rid of the Renault would shake me, by the way." She rested the gun against his testicles. "Now, where oh where should I put the first slug?"

Blake said, "Definitely not there."

"I wish I didn't have to."

"Maybe you don't."

She shook her head. "If I say I'm going to do something, I do it."

"All I did…"

"All you did," she said, shoving the gun in his belly, "is waste my time. I needed someone on my side in Louisiana. The only family I got left is shit. You were the one. And you left me. You left me for some bullshit nostalgia trip about nasty bitches from your past you seem to think you're going to hook up with again."

He closed his eyes. This woman had been sent by the cosmos to adjust the books. Before he said goodbye to the world, however, he wanted to pull one last pin from the Big System. He said, "I'm not the only villain in this town."

Don Stinson stood at the edge of the roof. He swept his hand across the parade of high-priced cars fleeing the premises. Without looking at Blake and Felicia, he said, "Unbelievable, unbelievable. Just unbelievable..." He took a sip from his drink and continued. "I send those buffoons down there with Ethan and they can't make one tiny, insignificant nuisance disappear. Worthless, worthless, worthless."

Felicia showed him the .38 and Blake told him to go quietly. The rich man must have assumed someone would come to his rescue. He didn't look like he'd ever had to defend himself. Not in a fair fight. If a hired thug couldn't eradicate a troublemaker, he could always bend the law to his favor, get someone tossed in prison on a bogus charge. Maybe he'd pull strings with the media, smear an enemy in the public eye. Results would be the same— death, figuratively or literally.

They led him down the other stairwell, across the bridge to Sarasota, and finally to the Chevy Volt Felicia had, apparently, borrowed from her uncle's crooked rental outfit. As they helped him onto the vehicle's cramped rear seats, Blake said to Felicia, "How long you been on my tail?"

"Since the day you left Metairie." She winked. "I saw what you were into. I had to see how you got yourself out of it."

He sat in the passenger side. The car smelled like Felicia's candy-scented perfume. "Pretty clever, eh?"

She secured her seatbelt and started up the car. Mary J. Blige played on the stereo. Felicia said, "You think you solved anything?" She laughed. "You can't ever return to Indianapolis."

"Why would I want to?"

She merged with the traffic of wealthy perverts fleeing the castle. "You can't escape Indianapolis. You can't get over the past, Blake. You're one of these dinosaurs who gets ulcers when you hear about people giving their kids participation trophies."

"Participation trophies are stupid."

"I know, I know. They don't teach the kids some ancient Darwinian concept of kill or be killed," she said. "The world ain't like that anymore. At least, that's not what the majority wants."

"Masses are stupid." He pulled up his nose. "That's always been the case."

"None of that matters." She turned onto Tamiami and headed toward Raro Key. "You got to flow with the movement of people or get trampled. Doesn't matter whether you agree with the new age or not. Natives didn't like Europeans swarming their land. Didn't matter. Rednecks don't like Mexicans coming over the border. Doesn't matter. Time goes on. You try and fight it, you're no different than a t-rex flapping its useless arms in a tar pit."

Don Stinson cleared his throat. "I don't see why I have to listen to this."

Felicia adjusted the rearview mirror so she could shoot him a glance, her painted brows at sharp angles. "You're the worst of them all. Blood-sucking motherfucker lurking in the shadows, hoping these webs your kind's been spinning never get cleared out by the truth."

The rich man said, "You want to talk about history, little lady?" A bubble ran up and down the side of Felicia's neck. Don Stinson continued, "Little shits like you forever try to disrupt the natural order. We always find a way to put you back where you belong. Yes ma'am, exactly where you belong."

"That's kind of true," Blake said to Felicia. He turned to face the rich man. "But you won't be there to see it. Not this time."

Don Stinson closed his mouth.

"That's right," said Blake. "Nobody's coming to save you. No cops, no media, no government agency designed to protect the wicked. It's no longer about the Old Boys Club, Mr. Stinson. It's just about you." The rental car wobbled as the wheels negotiated the iron drawbridge to Raro Key. The eastern sky had painted itself aqua blue. Blake rolled down the window to let in the cool air. "It's a good night for it," he said to Felicia.

She smiled. "We'll see how you feel in a little bit." She wound through Moonlight Pass and pulled into the parking lot by the beach.

Don Stinson made a fuss when they tried to pry him from the back seat. A reality he'd never known before must have sunk in: All the money in the world couldn't solve the riddle of mortality. Blake asked for Crystal. "I'll clock him one time with the gun," he said.

Felicia refused. "Just drag him. He'll make the right decision."

He did as she told him. He clamped his hands around Don Stinson's left ankle and yanked him from the car. The rich man's head bounced off the ground as Blake scraped him across the rough, artificial surface. Pebbles punctured Don Stinson's forehead. Blood trickled in tiny rivers down his face. He held out his hands and said, "All right, all right."

They followed him through the arch, through Lonesome Cowboy Bill's, which appeared to have been abandoned. The television no longer sat on the bar. The tables and chairs had been shoved into the corners. Only the rainbow-colored parrot remained behind the counter. The bird hopped and skipped and said, *Death of us, death of us.* It stood still for a moment and studied Don Stinson. It nodded twice and said, *Death of us all.*

On the beach, a cluster of hippies slept near their drums and torches. Two young men walked around the circle of unwashed youth, each carrying a spear fashioned from poles used to secure beach umbrellas to the ground. They stopped when they saw Don Stinson stumbling toward them. Tears betrayed their anger. One of them pointed his plastic spear at the rich man. "Why's *he* here?"

Blake threw Don Stinson toward the blood-stained iron clamp normally reserved for sheep. He put his foot on the rich man's neck and leaned on him while he prepared the collar. He secured the rich man and told the hippies to start drumming. Young men and women rubbed sleep from their eyes, executed doubletakes as they drank in the sight of Don Stinson, struggling to remove the collar around his neck. They whispered to each other as they set up their sacrificial star of torches. The drummers began a meandering rhythm as their rage at Don Stinson's invasion of Mozo's island blossomed into an energy. The beat increased and a lone woman in tan shorts and a turquoise tank top danced in time with the drumming. Leaves on the trees in the swamp rustled and the Caddie-sized alligator stomped from the darkness, producing a ferocious huffing sound, like a dump truck clearing its throat. As it approached the circle, the dancing woman twirled behind the drummers. The beast slowed between the torches and stared at its offering.

Don Stinson looked no different from the sheep, slamming his head into the sand as he tried to loosen the collar. He blubbered on about life being unfair. "What did I do? What did I ever do?" He pleaded with the hippies. He turned his attention to Felicia. "Surely, surely," he said, "*you* know this is crazy."

"Welcome to Raro Key," said Blake.

The alligator lunged for Don Stinson. The rich man tried to roll out of the monster's way. The alligator sunk its claws into the rich man's head and lifted itself to dig its snout into his torso, slicing into his flesh and whipping its neck back and forth, ripping Don Stinson in two. His eyes bugged as he gurgled his final screams. Blood gushed from his mouth and choked him as life vanished from his eyes. The alligator sectioned his torso and swallowed it in gulps. A stubborn crunch echoed louder than the drums as the beast snapped Don Stinson's skull between its jaws.

Only Felicia appeared upset by the carnage. The hippies looked satisfied. Blake felt nothing. He'd expected something cosmic, perhaps a comet, streaking across the gulf sky, signaling a hefty chunk of evil had been properly disposed. But the universe didn't care. He knew that. He'd known that the night he'd walked across the beach, following one of the young women to the drum circle, rationalizing the necessity of heaven. The *idea* of heaven. The belief might have been healthy for the psyche, for the soul, but it did not satisfy the nagging voice of reason, a plague the West had put upon the rest of the world, smashing beautiful mythologies and moral systems in favor of a cold, cynical order allowing nothing like magic to season the lives of the doomed.

Felicia asked him where he wanted it.

For a moment, he thought she meant sex. It had been too long since the last time he'd gotten laid. Even at his age, he needed it at least once a week. He said, "Let's go to my room." He nodded toward the building across the street.

"Sure thing," she said.

On the walk through the bar and the parking lot, reality arrived as Felicia reloaded the revolver. Blake said, "You didn't mean…" He smacked his hands together.

"Are you stupid?" She sounded like Chelsea Farmer. Like Lita Fisher. Like every woman who'd ever tried to jam a clue into the dense clump of putty between his ears.

"You don't have to do this." He spoke in a condescending tone, as though his sounding like a father might change her mind.

She talked of honor, how she'd marked him for the grave and had no choice but to follow through. Easy enough for him to agree with, on a conceptual level. Then she added, "I'm doing you a favor. Blake Ness. Lester Banks. Whoever you are. You don't belong in this world. I'm not sure you ever did. You sure don't belong here anymore. You're what the educated folks call an anachronism—a relic. Once upon a time, a man like you might have ruled the world. This is the age of enforced compassion, however. The exact opposite of what you represent. The individual is scorned, the collective is embraced."

They crossed the street. Blake turned his head from side to side. He considered fleeing.

Felicia said, "Have some dignity, lover." She aimed Crystal at him. "You run, I'll make it painful."

They rounded the building and climbed the tough, iron fire escape. Blake felt the muscles in his legs move with each step closer to the second floor. He'd never considered the beauty with which the joint in his knee had been constructed. He imagined diagrams he'd seen in textbooks. In doctor's offices. In massage parlors. The names of the parts didn't come to him. He'd never taken the time to learn them. How moronic, not appreciating this miracle of nature. Joints, muscles, tissue, operating together to sustain the briefest glory. He said, "You ever think about your breathing?"

"You know I do yoga twice a week." She used the gun to direct him through the door to the second floor.

He led her to his room. Despite construction vehicles parked in a half-circle outside his window, waiting, like vultures, to tear down history and replace it with a golf course or something equally useless, the contents of his apartment remained untouched. He went to the dresser and opened the bottom drawer. Felicia stomped her foot.

"The hell do you think you're doing?" She rushed over and examined the empty drawer.

"I thought, for a minute, my money was still there," he said. "I figured I might as well give it to you."

"You think I didn't take it when I went through your car? I'm going to get up from under my uncle's thumb. Going to live a clean life. Without all that shit I had to do to stay afloat. Without my uncle. Without my family. Without *you*."

Well, at least someone he respected would have his minor fortune. His taste of power. He addressed the ghost, "Haven't heard from you through all this."

She asked him who he'd spoken to.

He told her everything that had happened since he'd arrived on Raro Key. Maybe he thought the delay might change her mind. He tapped the transistor radio and said, "Connell Riggins, he controls, well, his ghost, that is, controls the radio."

Felicia raised Crystal, nudged the barrel against his skull. "You need this worse than I imagined."

"No, no, look…" He picked up the radio's power cord, plugged into a grime-coated socket in the wall, and said, "How could the radio operate without electricity?" And holding the chord in his hand, realizing the radio had always been plugged in, that he'd conveniently forgotten that he'd turned it on every night, that absolutely nothing he believed could be considered reliable, he looked out the window, past the construction vehicles, past the arch, past the bar, to the beach, where the fires from the sacrifice of Don Stinson still burned. "I wish I'd met you a lot earlier in my life, Felicia," he said.

Fireworks blasted in the sky. Four deafening booms. He no longer stared at the torches from a distance. He walked on the beach, barefoot, sand tickling dried skin between his toes. A blood-red sun painted the ocean a glossy tangerine. It had already cranked the temperature to triple digits. He still wore the fancy clothes he'd purchased to infiltrate Linda Lee's hangout. Sweat glued them to his skin and, for whatever reason, he could not undress. A monotonous pop ballad permeated the air from an unseen jambox. Same beat, over and over. Same, simplistic lyric, over and over. A young woman stepped in front of him, just a few yards away. Her hips swayed like a church bell. When she turned to face him, he expected to see Chelsea Farmer. She resembled, however, Lita Fisher. Nineteen years old. The age Blake Ness trapped her at in his dreams for two decades. The notion of hounding a non-existent person for the rest of time, he understood, did not constitute heaven. Not at all. The heat? The futility? He'd been rewarded the way scoundrels should be, sent to the place all the wicked, no matter their intentions, eventually wound up.

Alec Cizak is a writer and filmmaker from Indiana. His most recent books include *Lake County Incidents, Breaking Glass,* and *Down on the Street.* He is also the chief editor of the multi-genre fiction digest, *Pulp Modern.*

www.ingramcontent.com/pod-product-compliance
Lightning Source LLC
Chambersburg PA
CBHW032352280326
41935CB00008B/544